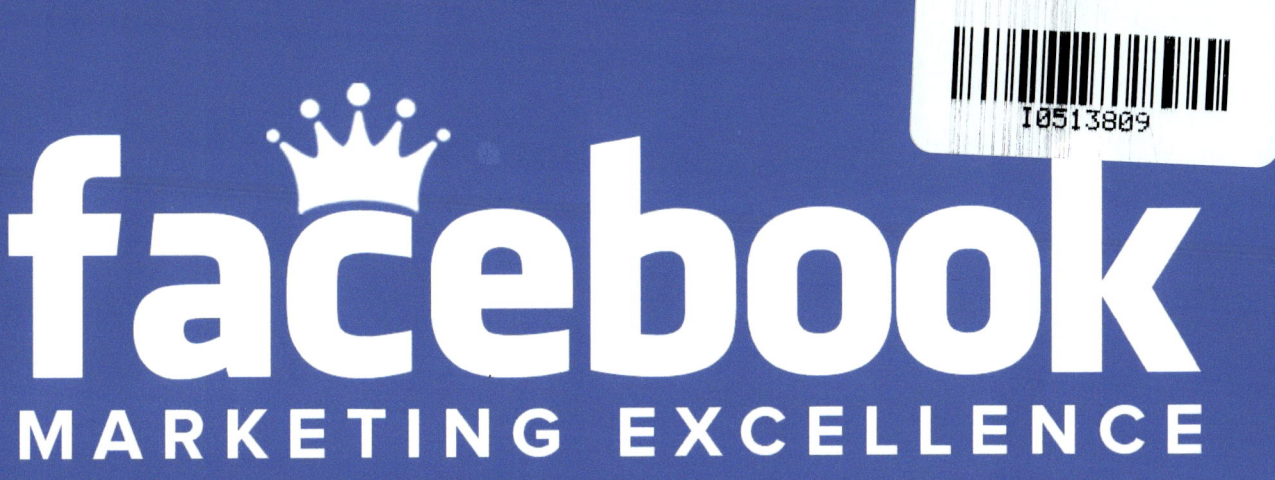

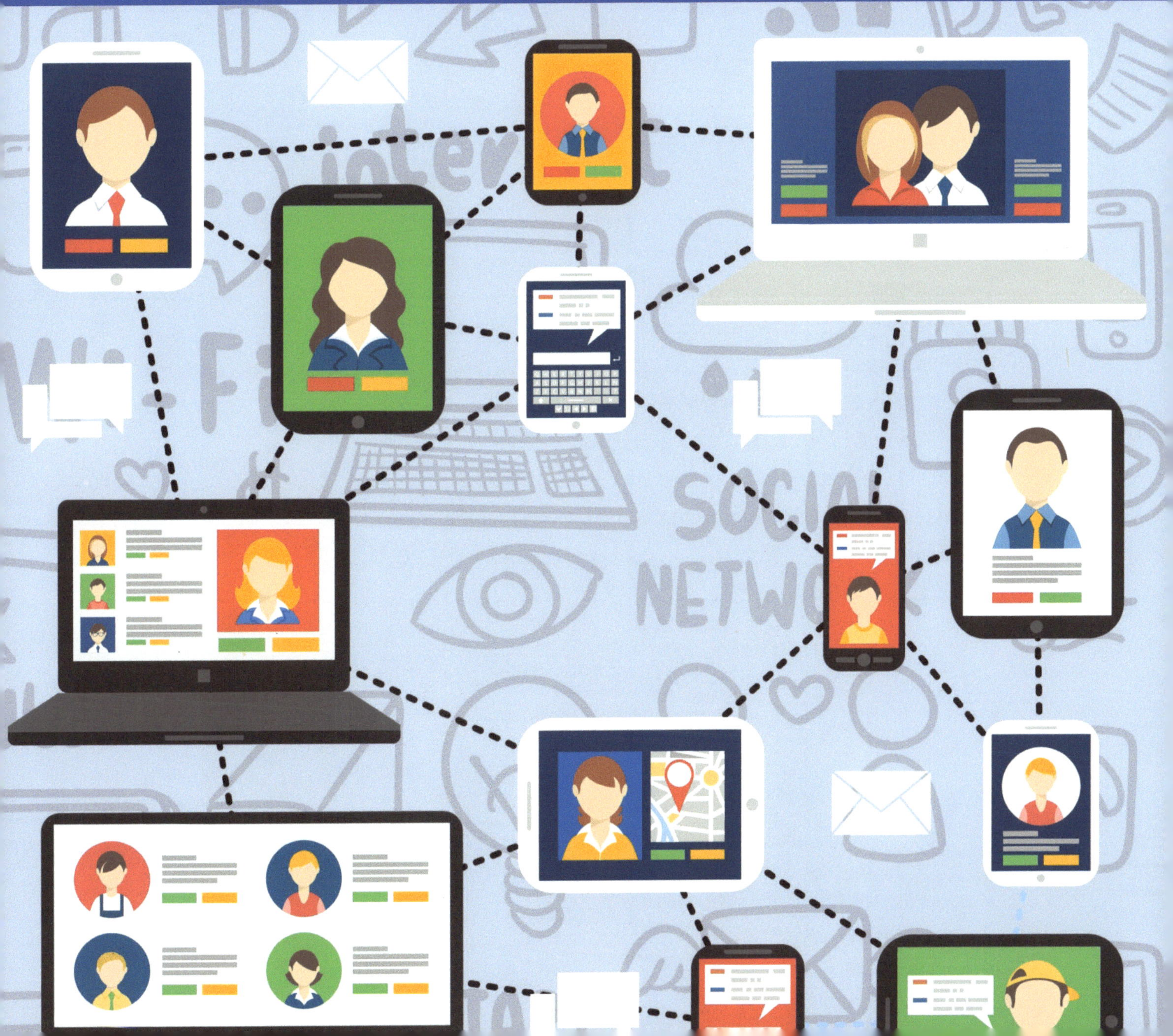

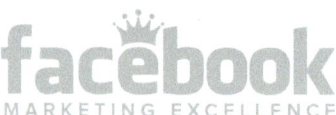

Table Of Contents

Introduction 4
Advertising In Facebook 7
   Understanding Bidding 7
   Targeting Your Audience Strategically 9
   Advertising Your Objective 10
   Facebook Advertising vs Google AdWords 12
   More Big Benefits of Facebook Ads and Your General Objective 14
Types of Ads 17
   Choosing the Right Facebook Ad 20
   Getting starting with ads 23
   Selecting Images and Editing Texts 24
   Targeting your audience 28
      Location 29
      Other Demographics 30
      Interests 31
      Behaviors 32
      Connections 32
   Custom Audiences 33
   Creating a Facebook Page 34
Top Tips For Effective Facebook Ads 39
   Use the Power Editor 39
   Use Content Marketing and Promote Your Page 40
   Find Amazing Content to Share That You Know Will be Successful 41
   Be Everywhere 42
   Play to Ego 43

CHAPTER 1

INTRODUCTION

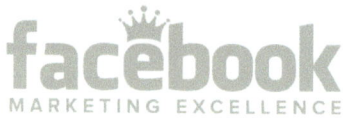

Introduction

Facebook is one of the most powerful platforms for any marketer to master and if you only ever invest your time and effort into *one* single social media platform, it should probably be Facebook. The impressive stats surrounding Facebook are by now old news but they are still worth repeating. Facebook is nothing short of the *second* biggest website on the net – right behind Google. If Facebook were a country, then it would be *one of the largest in the world*.

Facebook has 1.44 billion monthly active users, at least 72% of Facebook users check in every month and every day about 936 million people will check in. 65% use it daily. Among those users, the average time spent on the site per visit is 21 minutes.

In *total* there are 1,310,000,000 people who use Facebook regularly, which includes 680,000,000 daily users. Every 20 minutes, there are one million links shared, two million friends requested and three million messages sent.

All of this is really academic though – statistics like this are changing all the time.

All you need to know is that Facebook is *big* in terms of numbers. And what's more, is that those users are not just active on Facebook – they are engaging and taking part and they are sitting on the site for long periods of time.

In other words: this is pretty much the *perfect storm* for marketers looking for somewhere to access a large number of people.

And Facebook isn't just a big site full of lots of highly engaged users – it's also perfect in terms of the tools and features that it provides marketers. You have a *gigantic* number of people you can reach and Facebook gives you *all* the tools you could possibly need to reach the most useful members of that audience in a highly targeted way – this is powerful stuff!

A big part of this of course is Facebook advertising. Of course this is the paid option for reaching your Facebook audience and that makes it the 'premium' choice in many ways.

If you want the very most powerful tools for reaching people on Facebook, you need to pay for PPC advertising.

Don't let that put you off though – if you get this right then it will entirely pay for itself and you will make all of your investment back. We're going to look into how you should go about using Facebook marketing and advertising in depth in this e-book and in the process you will gain all the skills you could possibly need to start making the most of this incredible tool and resource.

Facebook advertising is actually incredibly nuanced with a ton of different elements. This is something that very few people will probably understand before they get involved – so read on to learn all about it so that you can jump in with the kind of knowledge most advertisers are lacking! By the end, you'll know more about Facebook marketing than 90% of those using the platform…

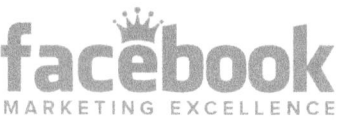

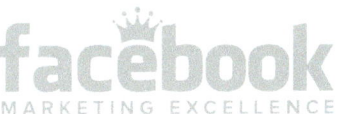

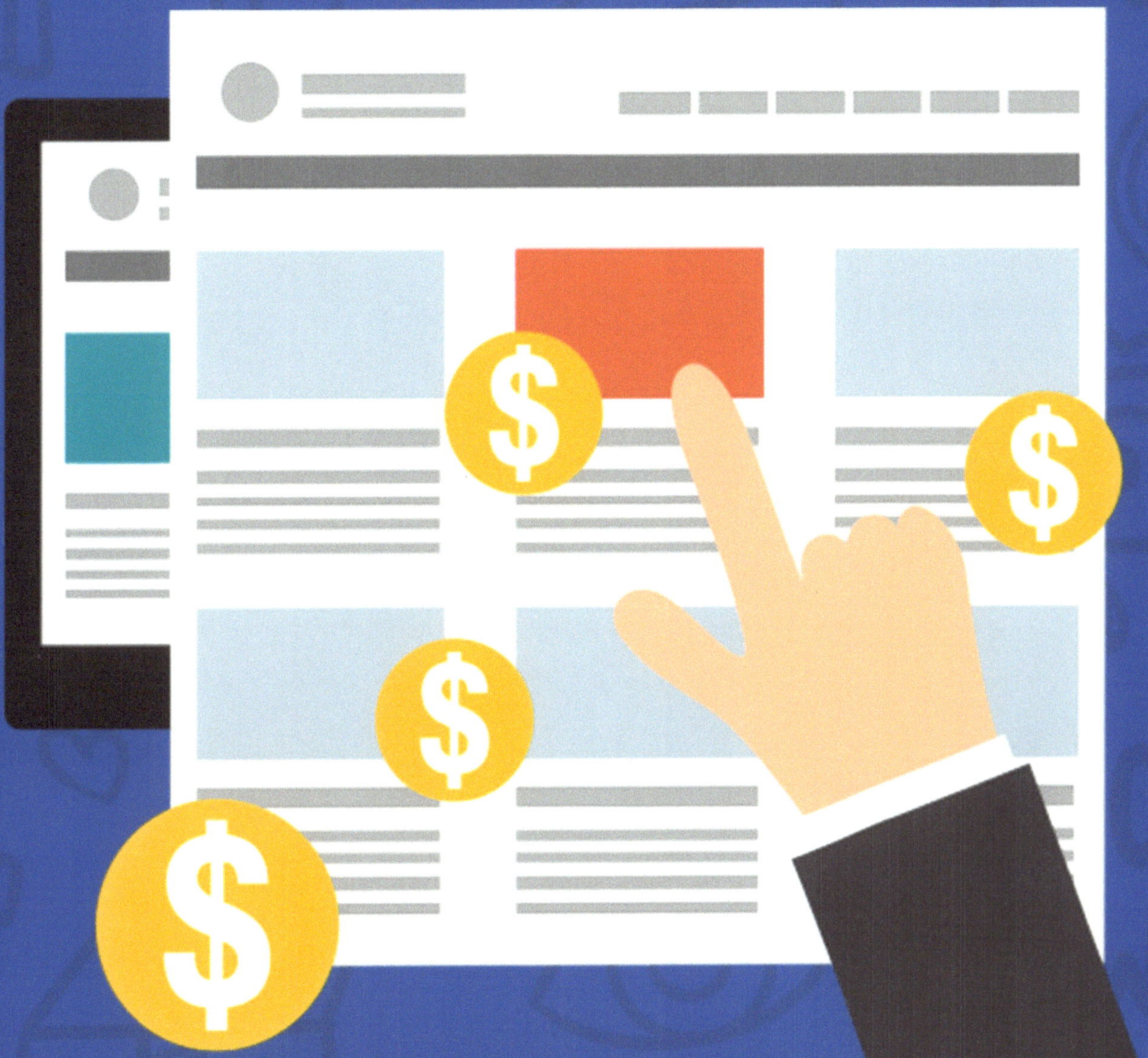

CHAPTER 2

ADVERTISING IN FACEBOOK

Another great advantage when it comes to PPC marketing like this, is that there's no set cost for your clicks and the minimum spend is tiny. This means that a huge company like Amazon can afford to spend hundreds of thousands of dollars on their Facebook advertising – while smaller businesses and entrepreneurs can also afford to pay for some ads and to experience with them. It's highly adaptable and this is a gigantic advantage when you have a limited budget or when you're just starting out.

So if there's no set budget then, how precisely is it calculated how much you're going to pay?

Essentially, this works on a bidding system whereby you will set your CPC (cost per click) and this will end up defining how often your ad shows.

Facebook wants to earn as much money as possible – as everyone does – and so the ads that they show will be dictated by who is bidding the most. Each time there's a 'slot' for an ad, all the relevant ones will be compared and the ones that bid highest will be shown most often.

So if you're willing to bid $2 for each click, chances are that your ad will be seen *a lot* but it will also cost you a lot. Pay just 5cents for each click and your ad will be shown far more rarely – but at the same time your overheads will be much lower each time someone *does* click on one.

Another important factor to consider when making this decision is your overall budget. You can set a maximum budget with most forms of PPC – including Facebook advertising – and this allows you to set a cut-off point and a cap on how much you're going to spend. This way, if someone were to click on your ad 100 times, costing you $100 that day, your ad would stop showing.

How do you calculate a good amount to set for your PPC and for your budget? We'll get to all that in a bit! What you basically need to know though is that this is a highly flexible system and that gives you the control you need to test the market and find the perfect price point for your ads.

Targeting Your Audience Strategically

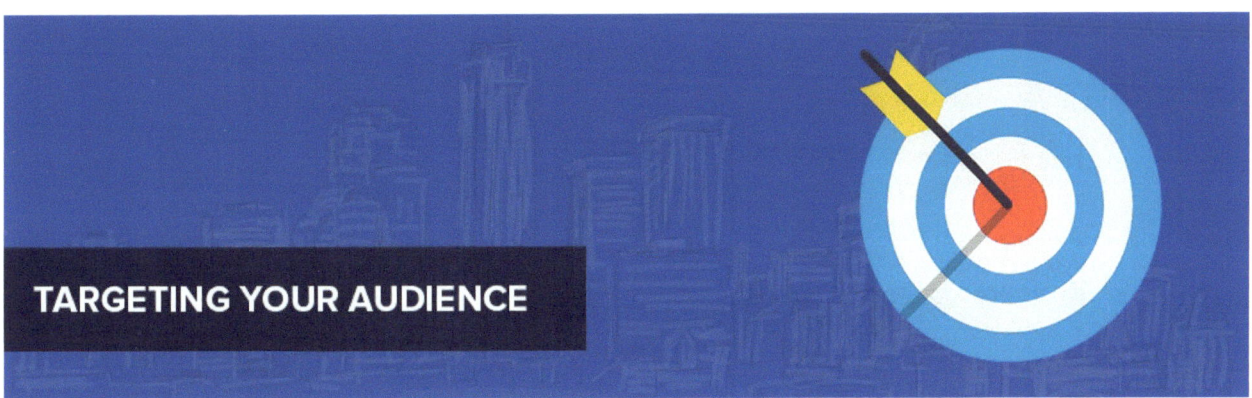

There is another *huge* benefit of Facebook advertising too – and that's the ability to target your audience strategically and very carefully.

Basically, Facebook advertising has the huge advantage of giving you access to *huge* amounts of information about each member. Users on Facebook will usually share details such as their age, their profession, their hobbies and interests, their marital status, their location and much more…

All this in turn gives you the very powerful ability to pick *who* you want to see your adverts. Would you rather that your ads were seen by teenagers? Or would you rather they were seen by women based locally who were in a relationship?

If you're wondering why this matters, then of course the answer is that it allows you to target your precise audience for your product or service. So say you have a shop selling wedding dresses; *that* is when you would probably want to target women in relationships (probably 'engaged') and living locally.

Meanwhile, if you were selling computer games from an eCommerce store, you'd want to broaden your ads to target everyone in the country (assuming you deliver that far) and you would want to target mostly males in their teens and twenties who listed 'gaming' as one of their hobbies.

This way, you drastically reduce the amount of people clicking on your ads who aren't likely to buy and you ensure that all your money is being spent on worthwhile and useful advertising.

There are many more options to explore when choose who to target your advertising campaigns at and we'll look at all those in more detail when we get to the 'creating your Facebook ad' section.

Advertising Your Objective

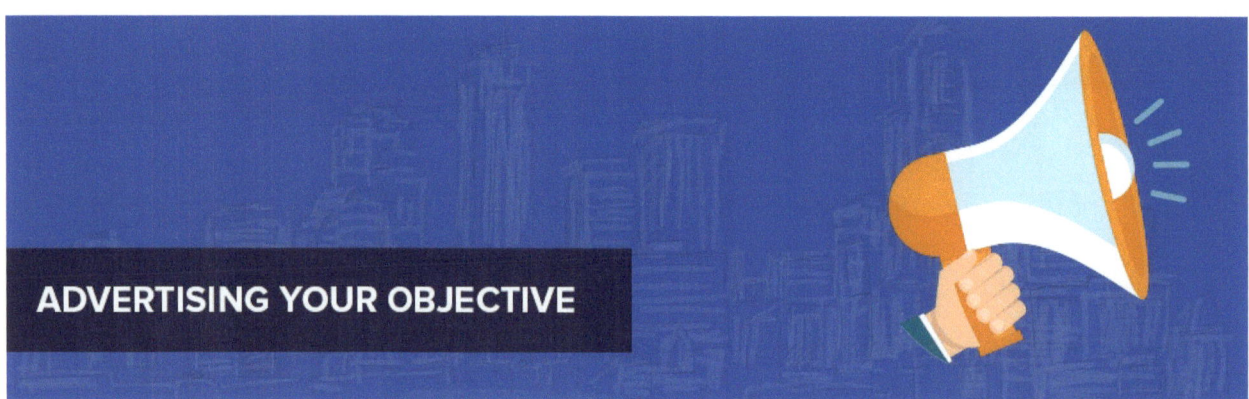

These are just some of the benefits and features available to you when you start advertising with Facebook. There are more and we'll look at them all in depth later on.

But to demonstrate the potential power of Facebook ads, let's give one example of how you might use them.

One potential goal would be to get direct conversions. In internet marketing lingo, a 'conversion' counts as someone going through with the action you want them to. In this case, we're going to say that that is clicking on your 'Buy Now' link and buying your $30 e-book on fitness.

The reason this is a brilliant strategy, is that you can sell $30 e-books with barely any overheads. Digital products like e-books cost nothing to print or deliver, so your only costs will be hosting and advertising. That means that if you can increase the percentage of people who actually buy your product after clicking on your ad, you can start generating a steady and stable ROI from your advertising.

So you'd want to create an e-book and probably you'd target people who were in their 20s-30s who would be most likely to want such a book and perhaps who listed 'the gym' or 'fitness' as a hobby (though perhaps not, depending on the precise angle of your book).

Then you'd create an ad that would show either in the sidebar, or on their home feed. In this ad, you would broadcast very clearly what it was you were selling and how much for.

This is where Facebook advertising can be a little different from other forms of advertising in terms of approach.

In the past, you might have learned that you save the price until right at the end – when you've already convinced the person to learn all about your product and to buy. This is the 'AIDA' approach (awareness, interest, desire, action).

In PPC marketing though, you are trying to *avoid* clicks just as much as you are trying to encourage them. In other words, you don't want people clicking on your ads unless there is *some chance* that they might actually be willing to buy. This is very important, as otherwise you are going to lose your ROI.

So now you will make your advert into a banner that very clearly says:

'BUY GROUNDBREAKING FITNESS E-BOOK FOR $30'

This technique will work because anyone who *wouldn't* want to pay $30 won't click. This means you can now afford to increase your CPC and have your ad seen more often. That means you increase your chances of being seen by someone who *does* want to pay $30 for your e-book potentially – and that in turn will increase the percentage of clicks that result in an action.

The objectives of your Facebook advertising then are going to impact heavily on the approach you use and will be intertwined with everything from your CPC to your maximum budget and ad design.

What we'll also see later is that there are also different *types* of Facebook ad – and which one you pick is very likely to depend on your objective too.

Now here comes the good bit: Facebook actually lets you 'set' your goals right from the start and the options they give you are fairly wide-ranging and comprehensive.

These cover:

- Improving engagements of a post
- Getting more likes for your Facebook page
- Getting more clicks or leads for your website
- Getting more installs for a mobile or Facebook app
- Promoting your event offer

If you're trying to promote an external page, then it makes sense to select the 'Website Conversions' goal rather than 'Website Clicks'. The reason for that, is that website conversions means that you're looking at *actual* sales or sign-ups for your newsletter rather than just getting people to your site.

The only reason you would prefer website clicks would be if you were making money from advertising – but there's a good chance this wouldn't be enough money 'per visitor' to make direct PPC advertising a viable way to grow your income.

Facebook Advertising vs Google AdWords

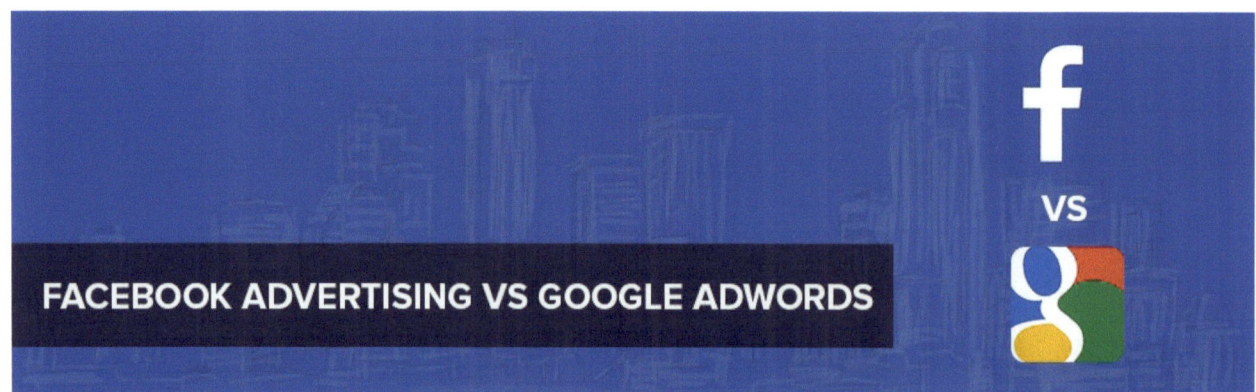

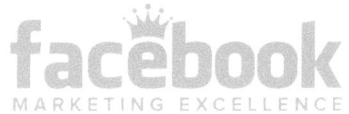

If you're interested in Facebook advertising, then you might also be considering other PPC models for your ads. There are numerous other options here from Bing, to Twitter, to LinkedIn and AdSense.

The biggest competition for Facebook advertising though has *got* to come from Google AdWords. Google AdWords is a type of PPC advertising from Google that places your ads on the SERPs (which stands for 'Search Engine Results Pages').

The idea here is that you choose a keyword you want to target. That means you'll be targeting a search term that people will use in Google when they're looking for something specific. If you sell hats for instance, then you might choose a keyword/phrase such as 'buy hats online'.

Now, your advert is going to appear above all the natural listings when someone searches for that term – with the caveat that it will have a yellow box saying 'Ad' next to it. Your ad might also appear on the right hand side next to the organic results.

Otherwise Google AdWords works very similarly to Facebook ads – this is PPC and all the rules are similar from the fact that you bid for your ads, to the fact that you only pay when someone clicks.

But there are some features that you benefit from in Facebook only and some that only Google AdWords can offer you.

For instance, Google AdWords does *not* offer you the same precise targeting of your audience. In other words, you can't target only people who have listed themselves as 'in a relationship' and you can't target people who have listed 'football' as a hobby (though Google is closing this gap in numerous ways).

At the same time though, Google AdWords has the advantage of showing your ad to people who are actively *looking* for your services.

In other words: when someone searches for 'buy hats online', you know there's a pretty good chance that they want to buy a hat. This means that they will be less offended by your advert appearing and offering them said hat and it means that they will be more 'susceptible' meaning that in that moment, they are more likely to buy. You should know that in advertising it is not only about *who* you target but also *when* you target them.

On the other hand though, Facebook advertising allows you to reach out to people who maybe *aren't* looking for what you're selling and this too can be very useful. For instance, it means that you can increase awareness of your product or brand even among people who otherwise may never have discovered it. This means you can broaden your potential market and that has a lot of advantages too.

Google AdWords also has some other nifty features though too. For instance, it allows you to combine your account with your Google Analytics account and that lets you measure how many ad clicks are actually resulting in buys – you can even work out your 'CPA' or 'Cost Per Action'. Google also lets you do things like 'remarketing' and using 'negative keywords'.

But then Facebook comes right back with more nifty features of its own – such as the ability to combine your advertising with a 'page' for your brand.

So which is better? That will entirely depend on your niche, your business, your product and your model. In 90% of cases though, the best approach will be one that applies multiple strategies and promotes synergy between them.

More Big Benefits of Facebook Ads and Your General Objective

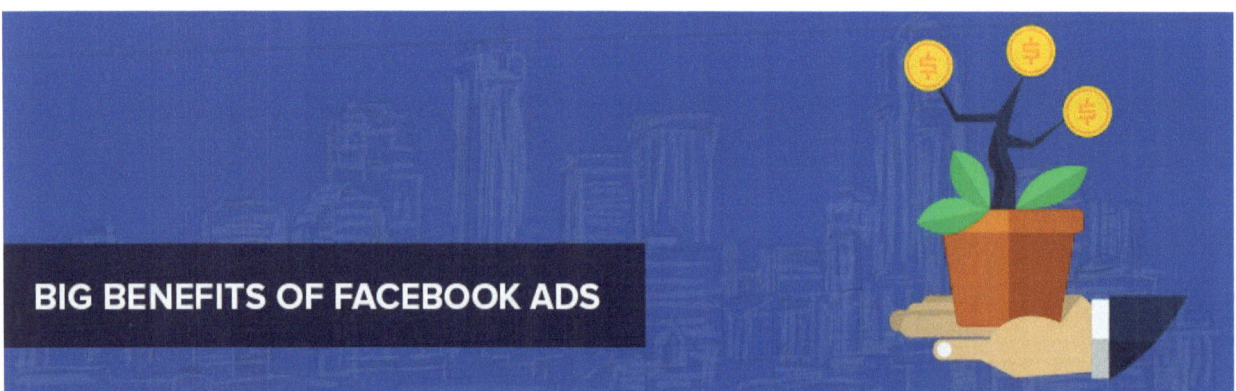

To really make the very most from Facebook, it's important to consider its individual strengths over something like Google.

We've already seen how Facebook lets you target users in a more precise manner and of course the way it lets you ad images and video and promote your page is good too.

But the *real* benefit of Facebook advertising is that it's advertising on a social network – and with a ton of powerful features that let you leverage this network.

One of the goals you can choose when creating an ad for instance is 'engagement'. Why would you be interested in increasing engagement? Simple: because if someone likes, shares or comments on your post, that not only means you're likely winning them over as a fan – it also means that that post will then be seen by everyone in their personal network.

What's more, the fact that they *like* your post/page will also be seen by all of their connections. And to those people, this might then seem almost as though they are advocating your brand. This is the 'social influence' factor and if you see that your friend has liked a brand, you will become much more likely to like that brand yourself, or to potentially trust them in future when you need their services.

And because liked and shared posts get seen by more people, that means that they can potentially go viral if they are creative enough and well enough designed. Your objective then is to recognize all this potential and to leverage it through smart ad designs.

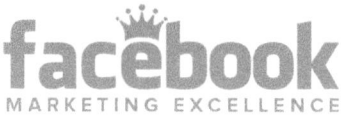

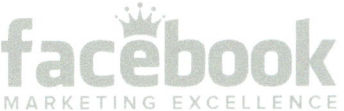

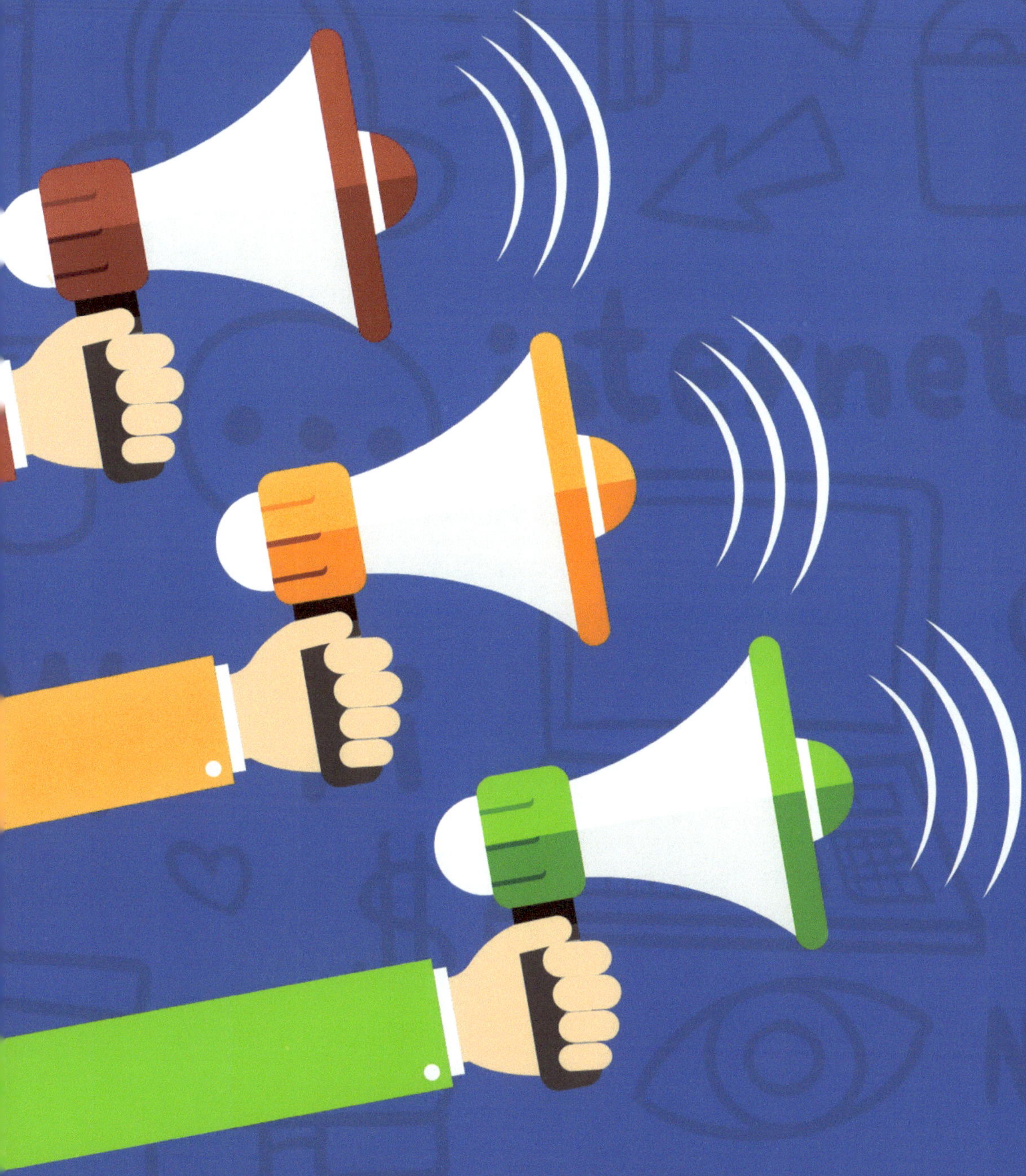

CHAPTER 3

TYPES OF ADS

but they are nevertheless a very affordable and effective choice that will be appealing to many advertisers.

Page Post Link

Supported Placements: Right Column, Newsfeed, Mobile Newsfeed

Page post links have become the most common form of advert used by Facebook advertisers. The idea here is to link an external website while at the same time getting 'likes' for your page. This type of advert is also perfect for combining with a content marketing campaign, which effectively means that you are creating regular content to try and build trust and authority in your niche.

You'll likely have seen a lot of page post links yourself when browsing through Facebook – and they will have had large images alongside a link and some text underneath. If you 'like' the post, you like the company's page rather than the post or image itself. If you click it, then you get taken to that post.

Multi Product

Supported Placements: Newsfeed, Mobile Newsfeed

Multi-product ads display multiple items on a slideshow type display that lets users browse and shop right from Facebook. This is incredibly powerful for e-commerce stores and means that you're really only posting one ad to promote a whole range of products. The movement meanwhile makes the ad more noticeable and engaging.

Page Like

Supported Placements: Right Column, Newsfeed, Mobile Newsfeed

This is an advert *for* your Facebook page, wherein you are trying to increase your number of likes so that you can generate a bigger audience to market to. Again you get a nice big image and a prominent 'Like' button – make sure to include a call-to-action in your text to encourage this further.

Page Post Photo

Supported Placements: Right Column, Newsfeed, Mobile Newsfeed

A page post photo can also be used as an ad which basically shows off a nice big image. It's not quite so effective for generating traffic as you get less space for text – but images will get you a *lot* of likes.

Page Post Video

Supported Placements: Right Column, Newsfeed, Mobile Newsfeed

Page post videos let you showcase a video. Again, these are good for getting likes and are powerful for video marketing. Creating a great video is rather time consuming and expensive *but* it can also be a very powerful tool when used effectively!

Page Post Text

Supported Placements: Right Column, Newsfeed, Mobile Newsfeed

This of course allows you to showcase some text but is a little bit of an anomaly when it comes to Facebook advertising. The problem with this one is that there isn't really much reason to use it: seeing as images are much better at grabbing attention and options like page post links let you combine both in a more effective manner.

Mobile App

Supported Placements: Mobile

This is an app that is specifically used for promoting a Facebook app. This type of ad can be used through the Facebook app in order to compel viewers to download *your* branded apps so that you can gain a direct way to communicate with them through a channel *you* designed. If your customers can order/buy through your app, then this can also lead to a number of direct sales.

Desktop App

Supported Placements: Right Column, Newsfeed

You may recall that Facebook also has its *own* ecosystem of apps. If you have built a branded app for Facebook, then this is how you can promote that and encourage downloads. Of course though, Facebook apps can only run on desktop computers and as such, you won't be able to promote these through mobile.

Event

Supported Placements: Right Column, Newsfeed, Mobile Newsfeed

There really are a lot of types of Facebook ad aren't there?

Events allow you to advertise events as you might expect. This can be useful for increasing interest for a company launch event for instance or a conference. This is one where limiting the geographical reach can make a lot of sense.

Offer

Supported Placements: Right Column, Newsfeed, Mobile Newsfeed

And finally! An offer advert is useful for companies that want to market a special offer. This works through your page again though and you'll need at least 50 likes to use it.

This is an interesting option because anyone who clicks on your ad will be e-mailed a code that they can then use in order redeem your special offer. It's great for encouraging sales!

Choosing the Right Facebook Ad

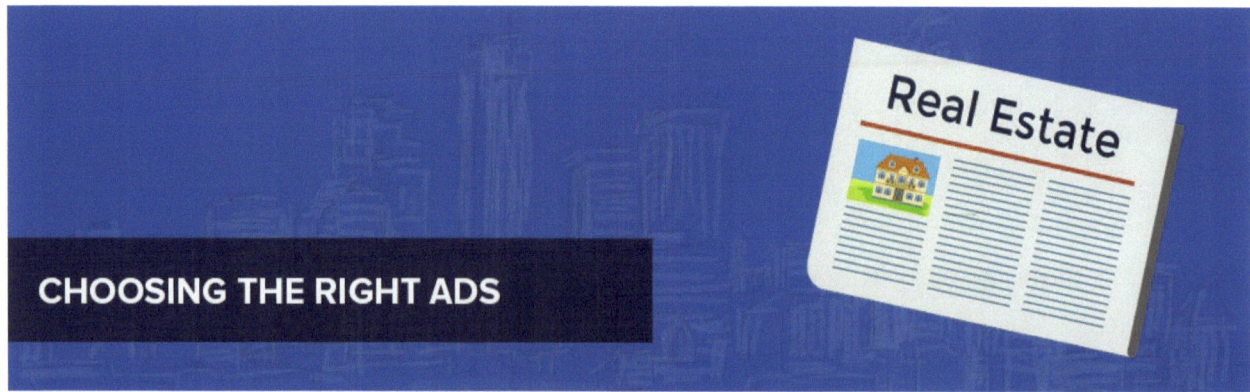

So how do you choose what will be the right type of Facebook ad for your particular objective, brand, product and/or goal?

As a general rule, you will want to use the domain ads when you're looking to generate direct conversions by selling a product such as an e-book. In the example we looked at earlier of the fitness e-book, a domain ad makes a lot of sense as it's simply displaying a product at a set price. These make sense in this capacity because you aren't especially trying to build your brand and because you will pay less for this kind of ad.

Meanwhile, the page post links make more sense for companies trying to build followers and represent a more long-term strategy. Gaining 'fans' for a page on Facebook can be a very powerful tool as it allows you to market to them more often and it lets you strengthen your relationship with them.

Unfortunately though, Facebook recently updated its policies so that posts on your page only reach about 2-6% of your fan base organically. Thus, you need to use a promotion such as a page post link or page post video. These still only reach out to your fans though, so if you want it to work well you'll also need to promote your page – and you can do that via the page like ads.

Finally, for ecommerce stores, there's clearly a big benefit in multi-item ads and for companies running events, event ads make sense!

Really though you won't know which ad is the very best for your campaign until you try a few. You may find that you're surprised if you compare the performance of a few different adverts, so experiment with them for a bit and don't make assumptions.

At the same time, you should also try to avoid thinking of each ad individually and instead think of them as part of a large campaign. For instance then, you might use a domain ad in the sidebar to generate some immediate cash but you may then sink this into some longer-term plans like using page post like ads to try and gain more followers for your page. Once you've managed that, you can then use page post links to grow your brand through a content marketing campaign and then start selling through your website. Facebook ads work best when you combine them into a single broad strategy and maintain synergy with your other marketing activities too.

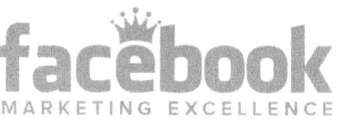

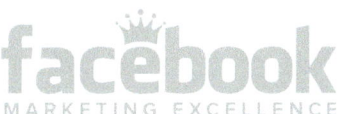

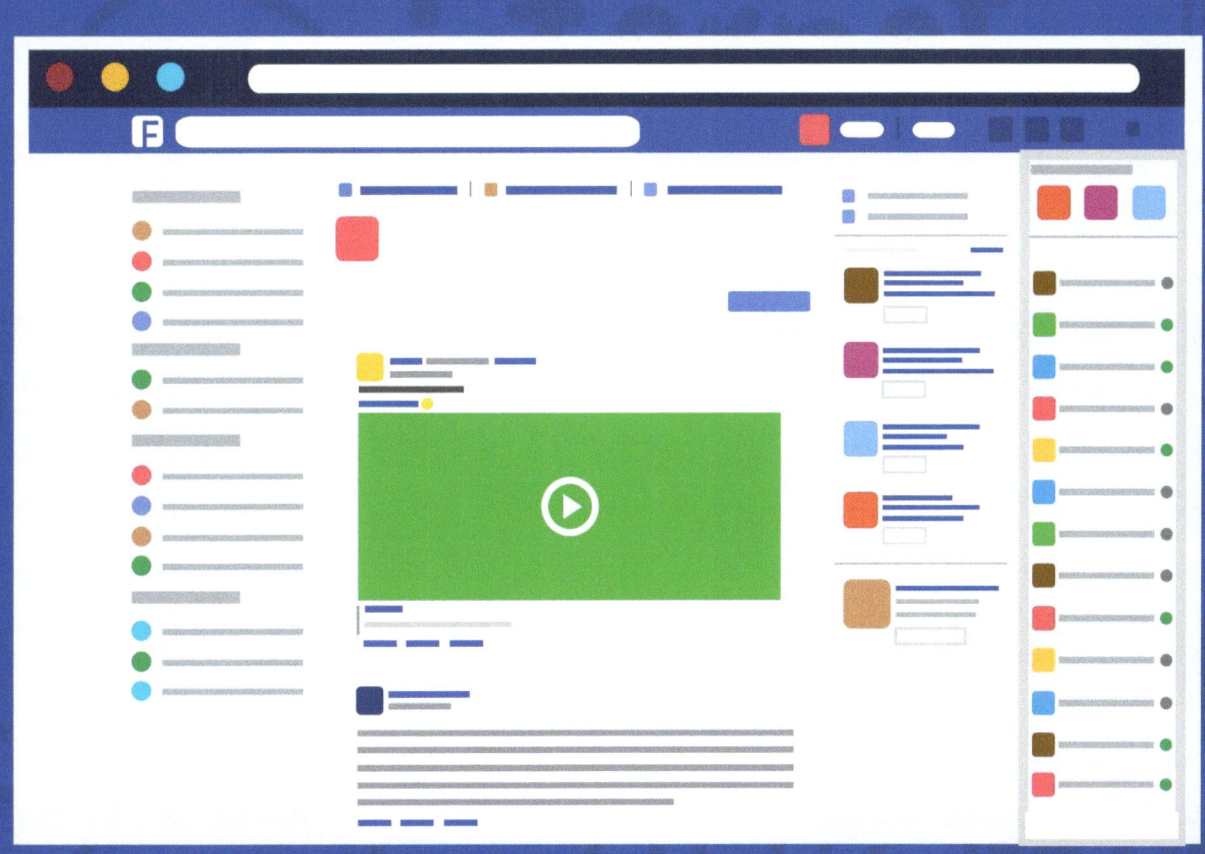

CHAPTER 4

CREATING A FACEBOOK AD

- App engagement
- Event response
- Offer claims

This will then define the type of ad that you will be creating so you don't have to worry too much about all the different types we listed earlier (though this is very good to know).

Selecting Images and Editing Texts

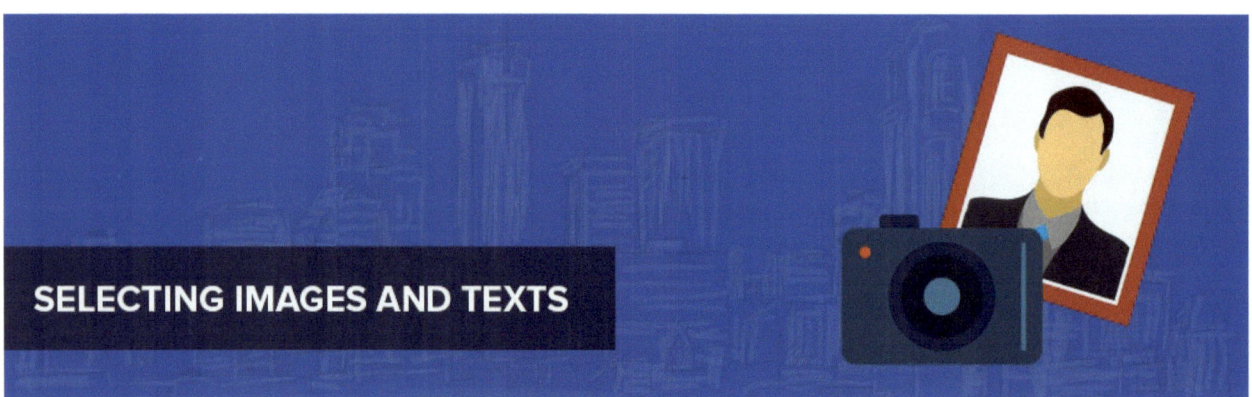

The next step will be to create ad images. This will mean uploading an image from your computer that you will have either created yourself or commissions someone to create.

We're not going to go into in-depth detail here on how to create images – but do bear in mind that an image is absolutely crucial for getting that initial attention, as well as for getting people to like and share your content.

Here's a strange truth that you might not have immediately realized about page post links: when people share or like these, they will very often do so without actually clicking on the link and seeing where it points! So they are essentially promoting something you shared without seeing it themselves. Why? Because they make a quick snap judgement on the content and then decide whether they expect to like it and to want to share it. After reading, they will normally want to get on with other things, so *looking* interesting is just as important as *being* interesting.

You can hire people to create professional graphic design from sites like UpWork (formerly oDesk), Elance and even Fiverr. Alternatively, if you have some vector software (such as Adobe Illustrator) then you can try creating your own high definition images. Learning photography and getting a good camera is also a good way to make your own images.

Another option is to find images in the Shutterstock database which you will be able to do when creating your ads. These look a little generic sometimes but they will also be guaranteed to be professional quality and to *look* like they belong as part of your ad campaign (which is important).

Here's the thing though: you must *never* use an image that you think is just 'good enough' or you might harm your brand and you'll at the same time be wasting time and money on ads that won't perform for you.

Make sure you are highly confident in the image that is with your ad and you think it can help you to get more clicks, more likes and more shares.

Luckily, Facebook knows how important this part of the process is and has provided a feature to make it a little easier. That feature is the ability to create ads and to test different pictures with them. Actually, it lets you select anything up to six different images and it will then try showing each of them for a brief amount of time in order to ascertain which one performs best for you.

For those reading who have ever tried selling a product through a landing page or squeeze page, this idea may be familiar – it's basically split testing. This means running small experiments to see what gets you the results you want most efficiently. It's worth making the most of, so make sure you're adding at least two or three pictures at this stage. Don't see it as an excuse to upload sub-par images though: everything you add should be something you would potentially be willing to use.

Ad Copy

Now comes the difficult part – adding the ad copy. This is what is going to be used to really sell your product, service, brand or page and it will be your best chance to tell people why they should care about what you're offering.

When you create your ad copy, you're going to be working with just a few fields. Those fields are: the headline, the text and the news feed link description (which is for those ads that appear on the news feed).

A little more information on each:

Headlines: These are 25 characters long and are essentially the titles of your ads. The main objective here is going to be to get people's attention and from there you want to get them to read further. This should be a little bombastic but should also explain in brief what your ad is selling.

Ad Text: This is 90 characters long. This is the body of the ad that will explain a little bit about what you're selling and why people should click to read more, like the page or do whatever else. You want to say something like: Yes, we're really selling these beautiful shirts for just $9.99. But hurry and buy while stocks last!

You can also add a 'call to action button' depending on the type of your ad. These have been shown to increase conversion rates, so if there's one that's appropriate for your campaign – use it!

News feed descriptions: If you are paying for a news link ad, then you can add a little more text – or another 90 characters to be precise. This is the part where you talk to your audience and say something like: 'Check out our great offer, for fans only! Like our page for more'. Or alternatively, you might use this section just to say a little about your brand.

Because this section is only available in the news feed ads *and* you get a lot more space for your image, these are generally the best choice for the majority of campaigns.

As for how you write your ads, bear in mind that you only have a very limited number of words to work with and that your audience will have only a very limited amount of attention: they didn't come here to be marketed to. As such, you need to make sure you keep your text short and sweet: get to the point quickly and try to choose your works efficiently so that you can say as much as possible with as few words as you can.

While you only have a few words, you still need to follow the advice that you normally get for promotional copywriting. We've already mentioned AIDA and this is certainly an important tool. You should always start with Awareness because you need to make sure your audience knows what it is you do – being obtuse never helped anyone.

Interest comes next, then desire and then your call to action. In this case, we can break this down into each of the categories:

The headline: Awareness

The ad text: Interest

The post text: Desire

The call to action button: Action

(This isn't a strict rule but can be useful as a basic structure)

The tough bit is getting your readers to be interested in your product and then to desire it in just 90-180 words.

To do this, you should again think as you would in any copywriting and focus on what is known as the 'value proposition'. The value proposition simply asks the question: where is the value in this product or service? Or to rephrase: how will the buyer's life be better as a result of buying/using this product? When doing this, you also need to ensure you are focusing on the emotional element and creating a real image in the mind of the reader.

So if you were promoting a binary options broker, what would be your value proposition? The simple answer is that your users would gain value because they would be richer as a result of using the service. Thus you might try to paint an image of them living the kind of lifestyle that they dream about: you can do that with an image of a luxury yacht, or you can do that with a piece of text saying: 'Your friends will be jealous of your seafront mansion!'. Now you have desire.

Another trick is to try adding in some kind of time pressure or another element that will convince them to buy more quickly. Insinuating that you have limited stock, or that your offer is about to run out will encourage people to act on impulse and to click the 'buy' button. This is important because actually the vast majority of things we buy that we don't absolutely need are bought on impulse. They are purchased as a result of emotions we felt at the time and if we're given time to go away and 'think about' the item, we will often come to the conclusion we don't need it. So get them to act fast by saying your product is available for a limited time only.

And remember too what we said earlier about sometimes not wanting *everyone* to click. If you are trying to make direct conversions, then think as well about how you can filter out the people who might *not* really be interested in buying.

Ad Position

Ad this stage you will also be able to choose your ad position. This is important as it is what will allow you to add more text if you choose a news feed ad and because it will drastically impact on the appearance of the image and the way the ad will be viewed.

Targeting your audience

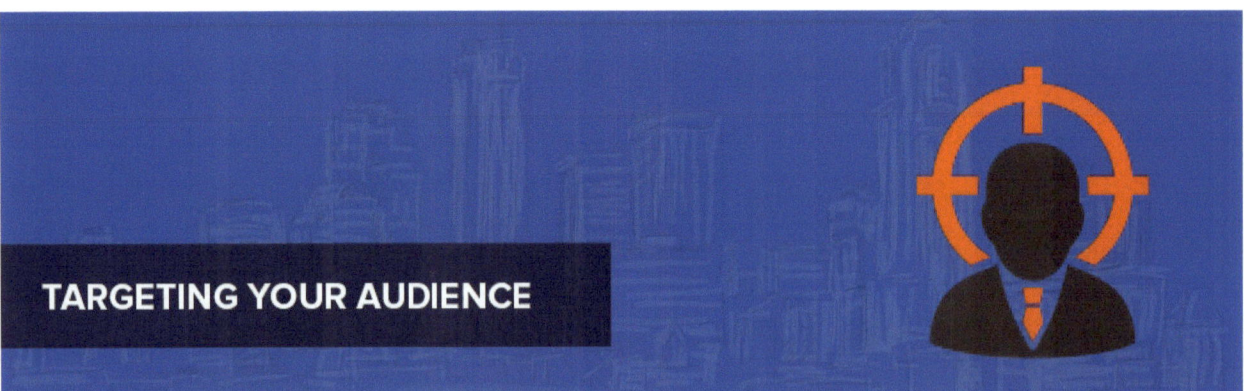

The next step is targeting your audience. We have already touched on this a fair amount but to recap: this is the process of witling down the people who will actually see your ad so that you are directly targeting the people who are the *most* likely to buy.

This is easy to understand in theory but when you come down to it, you will find that you actually have a number of choices and you need to think carefully about what you select for each one.

So to start with, you are going to choose 'demographic targeting' which means looking at the precise demographic.

To help you with this, try to imagine your 'ideal customer'. Ask yourself: who is most likely to want to buy your product? How old are they? Where do they live? Are they male or female? Write up a profile for them and imagine they're a real person.

Location

The ability to target your audience by geography is one of the most powerful features of Facebook advertising and is something you should use in a big way.

Of course the main types of businesses to benefit from this aspect will be the highstreet stores, restaurants and other businesses that can only be used 'in person'. E-commerce stores can sell to anyone in the world but if you're a hairdresser, you will only be able to work with customers in your area code. As such, why would you want to pay to advertise to anyone else?

Another big advantage of targeting by location is that it allows you to reduce the competition. If you are advertising to *everyone* on Facebook, then that means you'll be competing with a ton of other global brands. If you specifically focus on one area though, then you'll become a big fish in a small pond and your ads will be more likely to show up for a lower CPC.

For this reason, some companies will even decide to take a local approach to their advertising even if they *can* ship internationally. This way, they can focus on one area and become well known for that particular audience and then branch out later once they already have a strong foothold with a portion of the market.

The great thing about targeting by location this way as well, is that you can choose the area you want to target and then also choose how large you want the radius to be. How far are people likely to travel for your service? How far do you want to deliver? And how niche do you want to be?

Other Demographics

There are a ton of other demographics you can use on top of location for precisely targeting your audience. Two obvious ones are age and gender. Here you can think about the age of your most typical customer as well as their gender and then advertise to them directly.

But bear in mind too that you might think about this differently if you have different goals. For instance, you might not be so interested in selling to your 'typical buyer' but may instead want to increase the awareness in your other demographics in order to expand your audience. In this case, your question may be 'how can we better appeal to X demographic'? Or 'which demographic are we missing out on'? You may specifically decide to target elderly customers or women and create an ad campaign based around this intention.

Advanced Demographics

Facebook goes a lot deeper than just letting you target by age and gender though. At the same time, you can also target your audience by a lot of much more specific criteria and this can be a very powerful tool. Just click 'More Demographics' and you'll get the option to look at:

- Political leaning
- Life events
- Religion
- Ethnicity
- Job title
- Marital status

And more! This is an incredibly powerful tool because it means you can target a very specific kind of customer. Particularly useful for instance is the ability to target by job title: this will then allow you to sell tools that might be particularly useful for certain careers but at the same time it also gives you the ability to reach the 'decision makers' for companies. That means you can target executives and managers and use this to sell B2B services. Targeting by job title also gives you a relatively good indication of salary and you can use this to ensure you are reaching people who can afford what you're selling.

Note though that as you do this, there is a fine line to be walked. This is the line between being highly specific about who you are targeting versus still reaching a broad audience. Of course you don't want such strict criteria that only one person in the world is likely to see your ad!

Interests

Another way you can target your Facebook ads is by interests and this is again *immensely* powerful. Of course, when you target by interests, this means that you can pick only people who have actually expressed some interest in what you're selling.

Are you selling an album? Is it electronic dance music? Then look for Facebook users that have listed 'electronic dance music' or 'EDM' as their interest. Are you selling tennis rackets? Then look for someone with an interest in tennis!

Again you should write the profile of your 'average' customer. What are their hobbies and interests? What do they spend their weekends doing? What are their goals and ambitions?

Interests also gives you some other interesting possibilities. For instance, you can look for users that are fans of your competitors' products. It's a little sneaky perhaps but it's also genius!

Think as well about what interests might *lead* to an interest in your product. For instance, if someone is interested in virtual reality, they might also be interested in drones – seeing as they're both examples of quite advanced technologies.

It's worth doing a little research before you start filling out this section. Again, you don't want to go for obscure interests that no one actually has – so look around some profiles and see what broad categories of interests come up often. When choosing interests, Facebook also gives you the option to click 'Browse' and from here, you can look through the suggestions that they have to offer.

Behaviors

People aren't always entirely honest about their interests. If a guy is interested in 'My Little Pony' he may well not include that on his Facebook page. What's more, you might have forgotten to remove 'rock climbing' from your list of interests, even though you haven't been for 10 years. And anyway, just because you're *interested* in playing the drums, that doesn't mean you can and it doesn't mean you've ever bought a drum stick.

The point I'm getting at here is that interests, though useful, *can* be misleading. That's why Facebook also offers the ability to look at 'behaviors'. Behaviors include things like purchase history, intent, engagement and more. This is even advanced enough to allow you to target – for instance – people who are just about to go on holiday and who are currently browsing flights. This might be incredibly useful if for instance you run a hotel and you want to find people that are in the market for somewhere to stay!

Connections

Connections is another very interesting option that this time allows you to target people based on their connection (or lackthereof to you). So for instance, you could use this method to target people who are *friends* of your Facebook fans, or who aren't yet fans of your page.

One potential use of this is that it lets you try and expand your audience and gain new likes for your pages from people who may be more inclined to like them. This can also be an interesting way to potentially sell your items as gifts. For instance, if you sell branded t-shirts and your fans buy from you regularly, then marketing to their friends around Christmas may not be a bad strategy.

Another useful advantage of marketing to people's friends is that it means you have social proof. In other words, the people seeing your page will see that their friends like you and as such they will be more inclined to want to buy from you – thinking your products must be good!

As you can see, each of these different settings has a clear and obvious use – as well as numerous others.

Custom Audiences

Custom audiences is a fantastic tool for any digital marketers. Essentially, if you have a list of e-mail addresses and/or phone numbers, then you can upload this list to Facebook and then create a 'custom audience' to market to based on that list.

This is incredibly powerful for anyone who has spent time building a mailing list through their website. Normally a mailing list is used for direct e-mail marketing, which has the potential to be incredibly powerful. By using this feature though, you can advertise to your mailing list as well – giving you an entirely new way to reach them that will be more visual and that will mean you have the ability to 'be everywhere'.

Mailing lists are great because they are highly targeted. If you've been collecting e-mails through your blog, then everyone who has added their e-mail address will probably have enjoyed your content and will want to hear more from you. Thus, when they see an advert appear on Facebook offering them a special offer for a short-time only – they'll be quite inclined to click!

Creating a Facebook Page

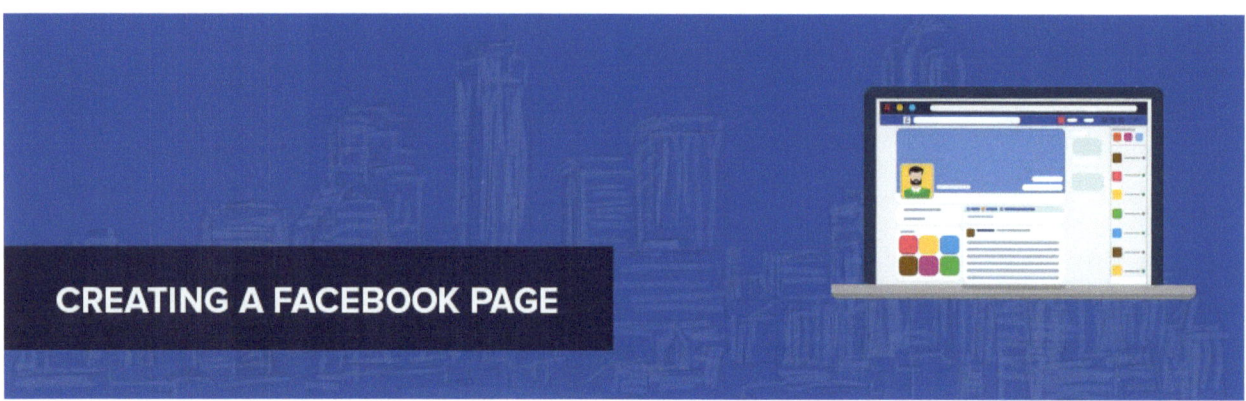

If you're going to be using page post links and page post likes, then you need to have a good Facebook page in order to tie everything together. This will allow you to gain a larger audience to market to and it will ensure that when someone *does* go to your page, they will have only positive experiences.

Creating a Facebook page is very similar to creating a profile page for yourself personally and you have many of the same elements: such as information, a profile picture and a cover image.

One tip here is to make sure you have strong branding that comes across in your page. A great logo makes a world of difference here so if you haven't already, invest the time and/or money into creating a good one. Likewise, consider using a writer to fill in your details and make sure that your writing style matches the tone of your business.

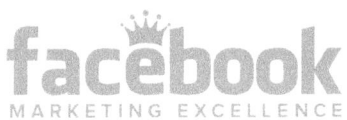

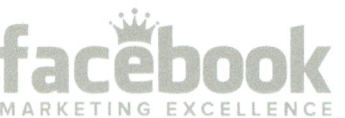

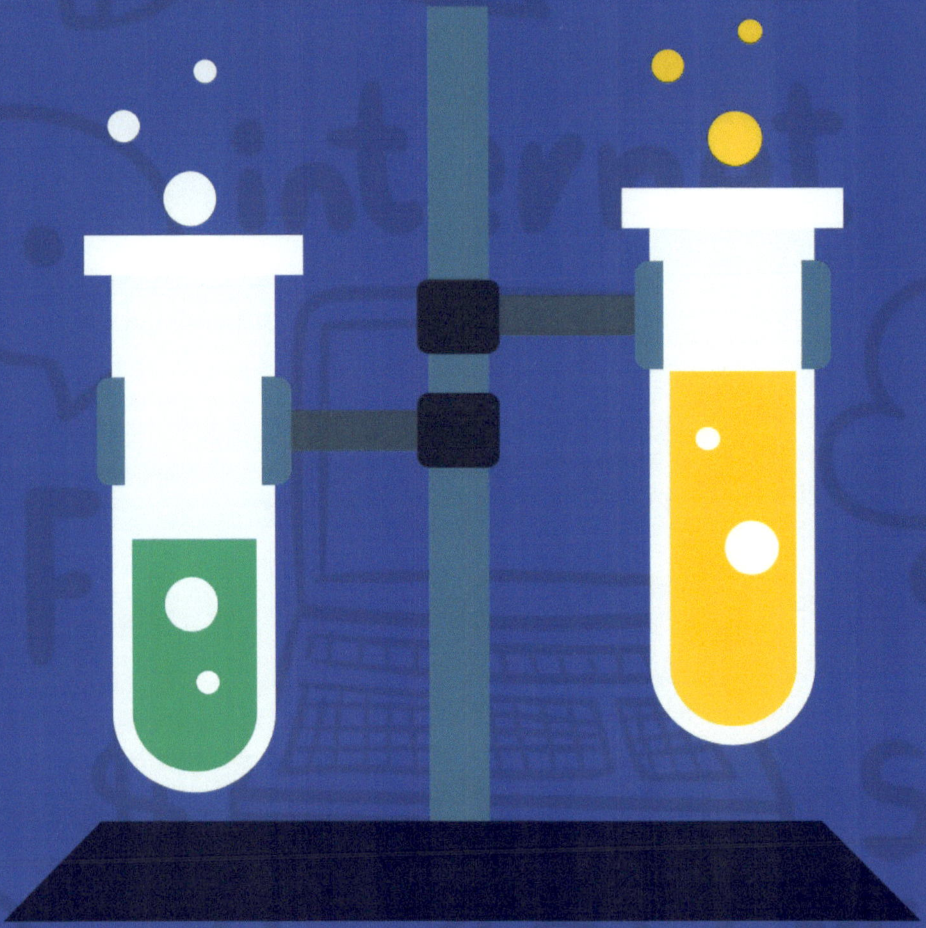

CHAPTER 5

TESTING, TWEAKING YOUR AD

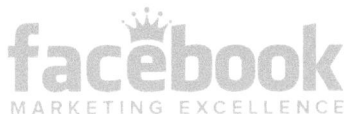

Over the data table on the left meanwhile, you can opt whether you want to see the stats for campaigns, ad sets or ads. On the right, you can select the timeframe you want to look at – this is useful because you can see how they're performing in the long-term versus right now.

For a more detailed breakdown, take a look at one of the ads or campaigns just by clicking on them. Now you'll be shown a graph that will look like a line graph and that will plot the clicks/conversions/likes of your specific ad over time. This is where you will be able to see the impact that a particular change had – simply log when you made the change and see how this impacted on the trajectory of your clicks or likes. Another way to do this is to make two very similar ads/campaigns and to look at which one is performing best.

An important figure to look at among all this data is the 'frequency' figure. This number tells you how regularly your ad is being seen by the same person. If your ad frequency is high – say above 15 – then this suggests that people have seen your ad repeatedly and have probably already bought from you or aren't going to. This would be a good time to try mixing things up a bit.

Advanced Data

If you want even more advanced data then click 'view report'. Here you will get a lot of raw data you can analyze and this will include such figures as your 'cost per action' which tells you more closely what your ROI is likely to be for a given ad. This can show you all sorts of clever things – such as whether your users are using the apps they installed.

Another cool feature here is the ability to view aggregated data. This means you can break it down to view data by age, by location, by sex etc. This is very handy because it will let you see where your ad is performing best. That way, you can either choose to focus your future ads on that group more, *or* you can look at why you are underperforming in some areas and at what you can do about that.

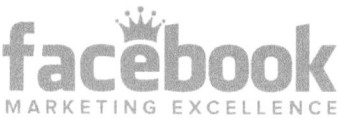

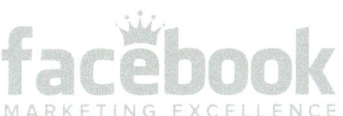

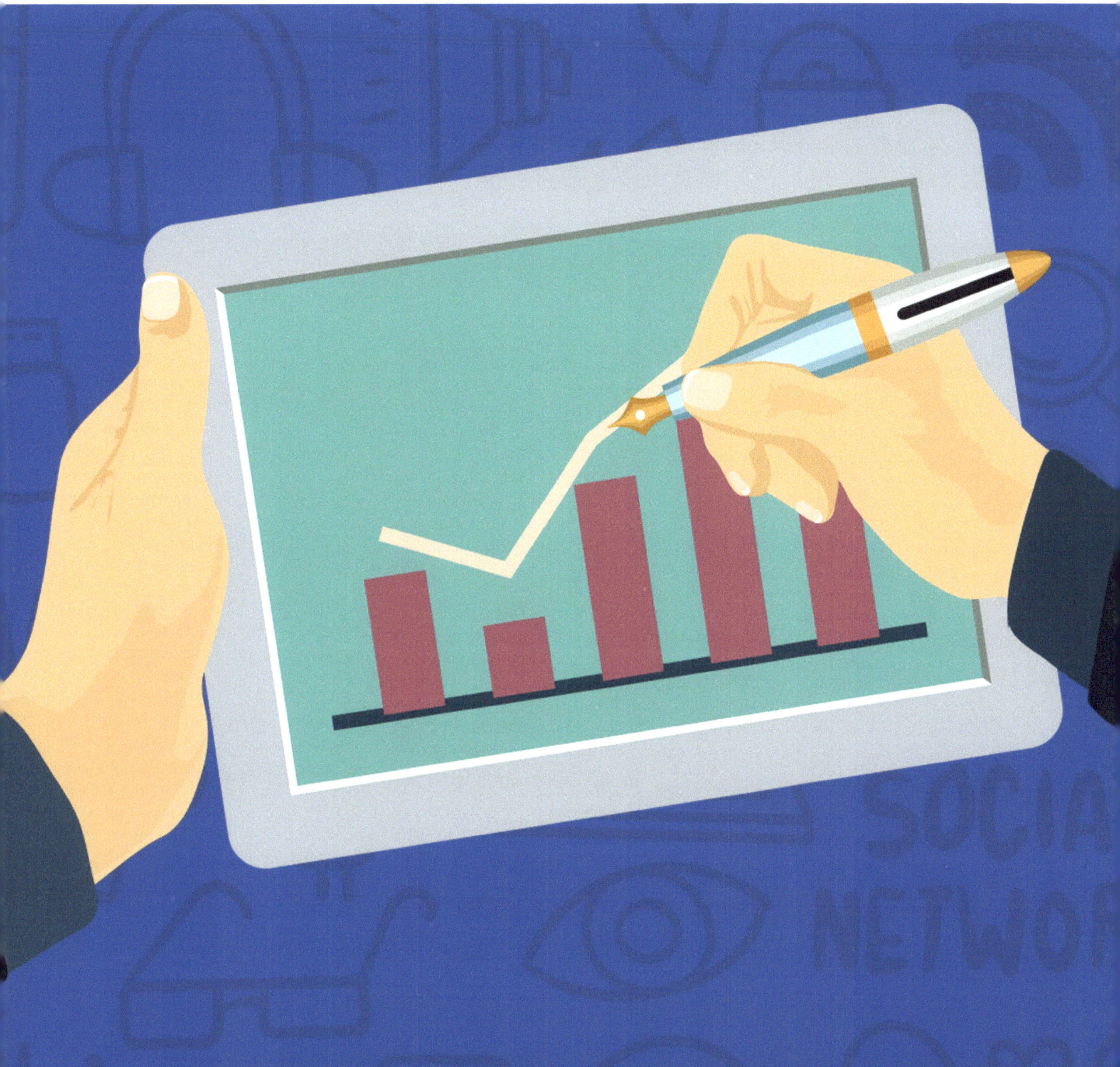

CHAPTER 6
TIPS FOR EFFECTIVE ADS

A lot of people reading this won't need the Power Editor. But for those of you looking to invest a lot of time and money, this can save you a lot of trouble!

Use Content Marketing and Promote Your Page

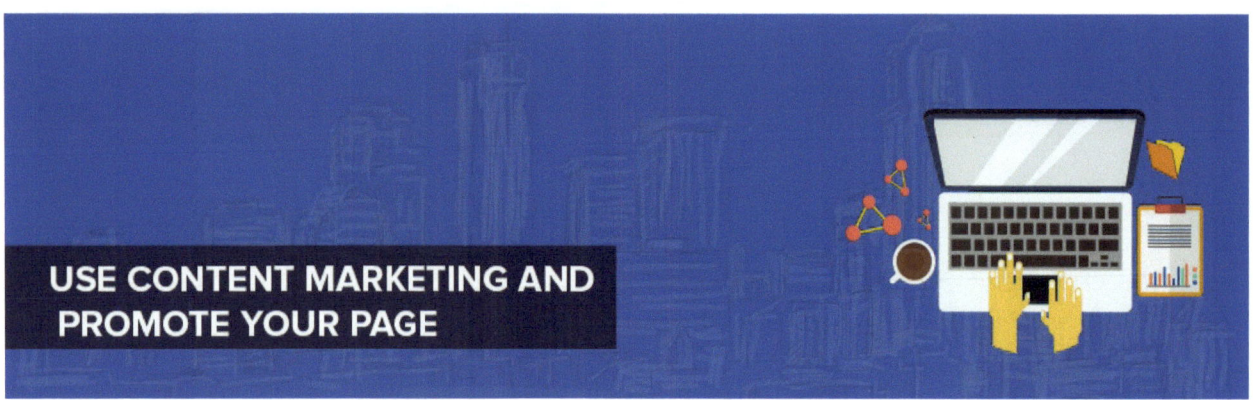

Facebook marketing and Facebook advertising both work much more effectively when you have a good content marketing strategy to back them up. Content marketing is the process of using blog posts, articles and other content to try and build trust with your audience and to get them to see you as an authority in your niche or industry. At the same time, content marketing is effective for generating likes and shares – because if you have a great article on your page, then you can encourage people to like and share it.

One way to combine the two then is to run a blog and post great content there regularly so that you get regular visitors. Do this and include the ShareaholicWordPress plugin so that your visitors can easily share your content to their Facebook pages.

At the same time, make sure *you* are posting your content to your Facebook as page post links. This way you can get more people to read your content – especially if you give it a good picture and a good title that sounds interesting. Don't be derivative – try to stand out and this will make your content much more likely to share quickly and easily.

You should also add a link to your Facebook page to your blog and to any other content you create (such as a YouTube channel). Ideally, someone will come to your site regularly because they find your writing interesting and they will then see that you've got a link to your Facebook page at the top.

If you're getting at least a few hundred visitors to your site a day and you have a visible and prominent link to your Facebook page on there – you'll find that this gets you at least a couple of new likes a week pretty easily and reliably.

Another tip is to add a mailing list to your content. A brilliant benefit of this is that all the people who sign-up to your mailing list will be *directly* reachable from then-on, rather than being reachable only through Facebook putting you at the mercy of a third party service.

At the same time, as we've already seen, you can actually use your mailing list to create highly targeted adverts and this is a great way to combine two different types of marketing.

Find Amazing Content to Share That You Know Will be Successful

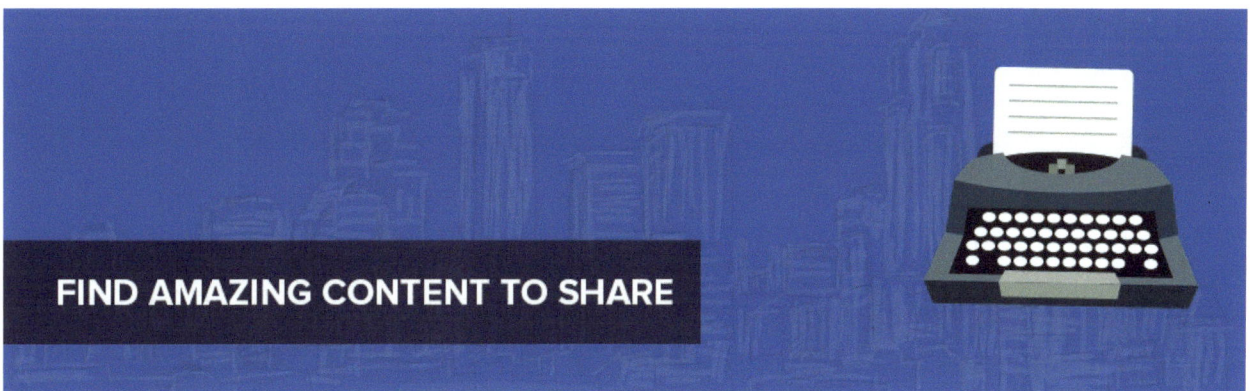

Not everything you post has to be your own. If you have a page, there's nothing to stop you sharing relevant links and interesting things you've found as well as images.

Why would you want to share a link to a site other than your own and *pay* for the privilege?

Simple: because if someone *likes* that post, it's your page that will receive the like. This is pretty smart – you upload 'Gangnam Style' just when it's taking off and by doing so, you get to receive all the likes!

Share a cute dog and you'll get loads of likes guaranteed!

That said though, you also of course need to think about how what you're sharing is going to impact on your brand – you need to cater to your target demographic and you need to stay 'on point' as much as possible.

The question then, is how do you find amazing content that you can share and that's relevant to your company?

One tip is just to follow lots of *other* people. This way you can see what's working for them and you can even *borrow* those things to use on your own page.

Another method is to use BuzzSumo. BuzzSumo is a tool that is specifically designed for finding 'trending' content and it allows you to see what's getting lots of shares and likes. Keep an eye on this and you'll be able to find inspiration to share through your own channels.

Be Everywhere

As mentioned early on in this book, it's important to think of your Facebook marketing in the broader context of your overall campaign and goals. We've already seen how it can work well with content marketing but at the same time, it can also be combined with influencer marketing, with SEO and with Google AdWords. We've seen that AdWords and Facebook ads are quite different – so why not use them to target different sections of your audience?

What's more, you should also work on other social media channels like Twitter, like LinkedIn and like Google Plus. Then, across all of these different platforms, you should make sure you are consistently using the same username and the same logo. Now, every time someone clicks on anything you've done, they'll be greeted with the same consistent imagery and this will help to tie all the strands of your business together and to reinforce your branding.

One old adage in the world of social media is 'be everywhere'. This is very good advice.

Play to Ego

The last tip we'll share is one of the single most powerful when it comes to making your ads a hit: and that's to play to ego.

What is meant by this? Simply that the most successful posts are ones that allow your readers to be a little narcissistic.

In other words, take into account the fact that most people share content on social media because they think it shows themselves in a good light and because they are *expressing* themselves.

Why would you 'like' a post on Facebook? Is it because you want other people to read that post? Or is it because you want other people to *see that you've liked it*. Do you like posts about black holes sometimes so that you look intellectual? Or posts about charities so that you look generous and thoughtful? A lot of people do!

And so, if your objective is to try and promote as many shares and likes for your ads as possible, you need to try and post things that people will *want* to share and that will make them look good. Another good way is to target a specific niche – such as people who work from home, or people who work out. That way, people belonging to those groups will likely share the content to demonstrate their continued allegiance to that way of life. Humans are a funny bunch…

While we might seem egocentric though, there is one other common reason that we share content: and that's as a form of communication. Again, this is why it can be effective to write articles that describe a specific type of person – because that way people will want to share the content with their friends who fit that mold.

When designing any ad and looking for engagement, ask yourself: would you be likely to click share or like if *you* saw it?

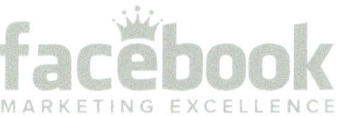

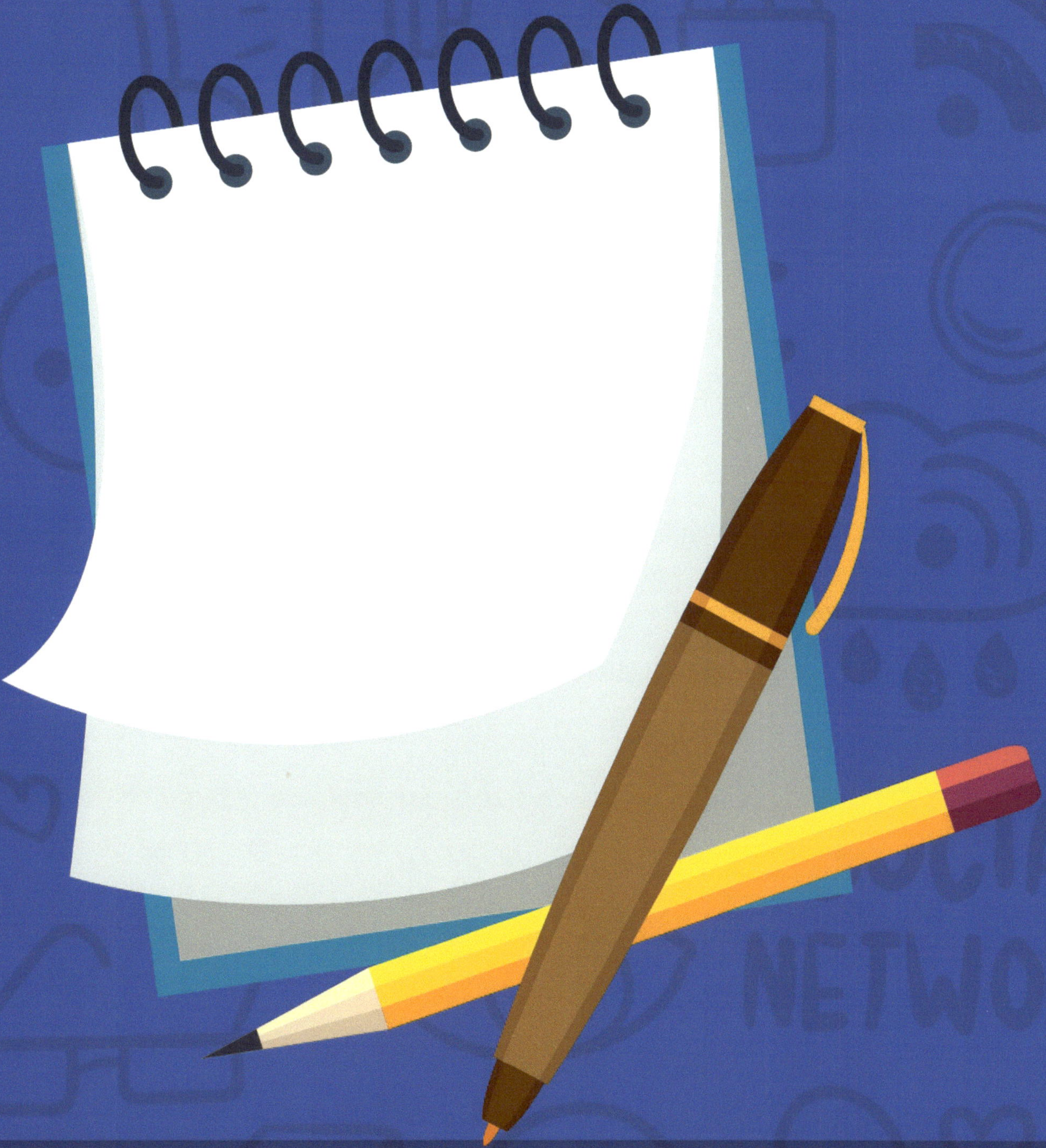

CHAPTER 7

SUMMARY

- - And more
- Choose two or more images to let Facebook find which one works best for your ad
- When writing the copy think AIDA and think 'value proposition'
- View your ads' performance in the ad manager
- And tweak the design occasionally to see how this impacts on your conversions
- Use Facebook Power Editor if you have a huge amount of ads
- Combine your Facebook campaign with a good content marketing campaign
- Use BuzzSumo to find good 3rd party content to share
- Share things that allow people to express themselves and/or communicate

And that's basically it…

So there's nothing left for it but to dive in. Good luck!

www.ingramcontent.com/pod-product-compliance
Lightning Source LLC
Chambersburg PA
CBHW040409220526

45473CB00004B/1180

A CineMagician interview with Movie Maker Brett Piper

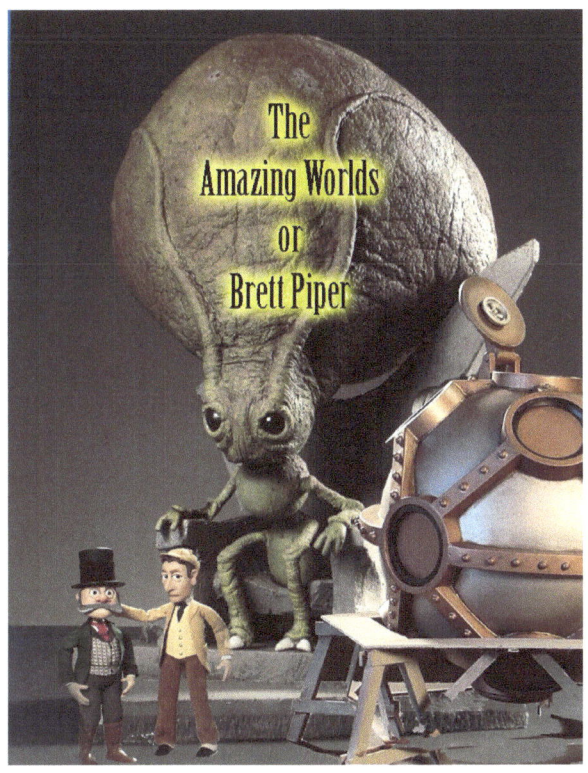

If you haven't heard of Brett Piper you need to re-introduce yourself to the world of Stop-Motion movie making. If talent was the measure of success, Brett is right up there with the likes of Willis O'Brien, Ray Harryhausen, Jim Danforth, David Allen, and Pete Peterson. In many ways, Brett's career is a bit like Pete's, lots of talent little money to work with so he pulls out the stops and burns the thinking box.

Brett's movie making endevors date back to his youth, but he got his first taste of 'success' with a movie called Mysterious Planet, very losely based on the Jules Verne novel Mysterious Island. This first venture into feature making actually got distributed in Germany and if you want to struggle past a really bad Russian narration you can watch the English version on YouTube.

While Brett has been involved in many productions, the ones you want to take the real time to enjoy are the ones he is listed as Director on the IMDB. You will find titles like: A Nymphoid Barbarian in Dinosaur Hell, Arachnia, Muckman, Queen Crab, and his latest Outpost Earth. While none of these have the lavish of multi-million dollar budgets, they all have the care and loving of a craftsman that knows what he is doing.

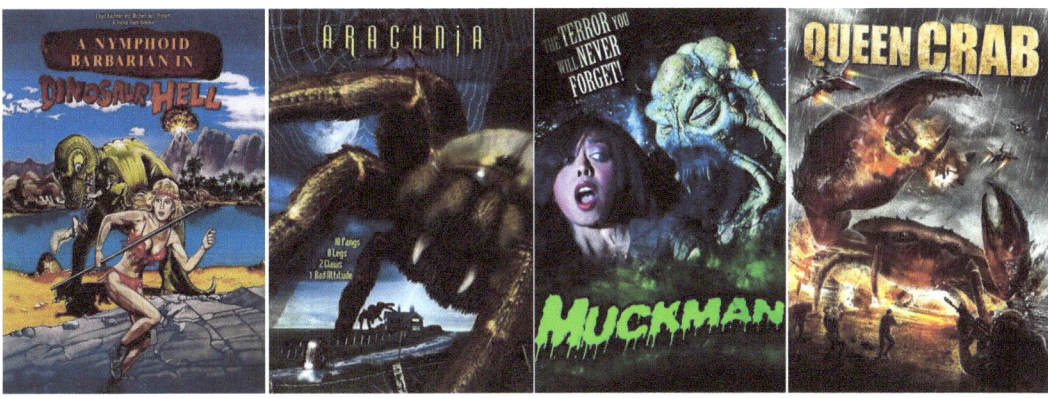

CM: What attracted you to movie making and how long have you been doing it?

Brett: It's very much the usual story. As a kid I was captivated by *Kong* and the Universal horror

CINEMAGICIANS

Volume 5   December 2017

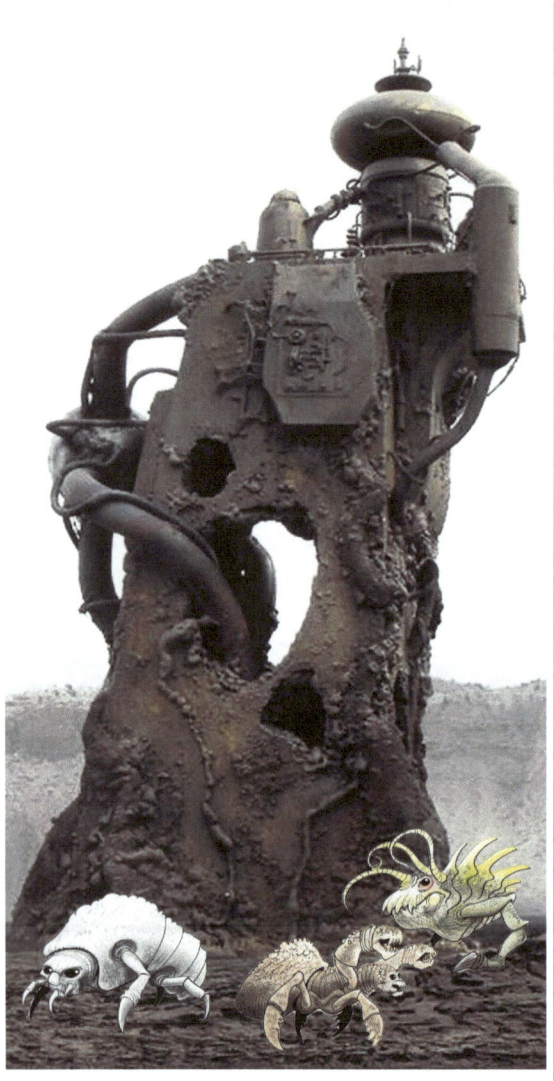

INDEX

The Amazing Worlds of Brett Piper ... 2

Morezmore Humanly Posable Armature ... 7

A Visit to the Zu-3D ... 14

PLATYPOSSUM –

The Journey ... 20

The Lost Forest/Last Voyage of the Lovecraft ... 27

Back cover art by Roger Koch

Edited by David D'Champ

CineMagicians Volume 5 December 2017 – A magazine for backyard movie makers. Published irregularly or when ever we have enough material to put together an issue. Which is basically when I successfully beat up enough people to provide articles. All articles are the property of the people who authored them. - ed series. Those movies were just magical to me. My friends and I used to renact scenes from them, and one day we saw an advertisement for a 8mm Kodak movie camera on sale and thought it would be cool to actually make our own versions of those movies. We pooled our money and bought the camera and the first thing we tried to make was a version of *The Lost World* --- in 8mm, on fifty feet of film, which runs about three minutes. It was a disaster, of course. I tried making stop motion dinosaurs out of clay but I knew nothing about lenses or depth of focus and they were just jerky little blurs. But I kept at it and gradually developed more skills and started making less embarassing movies, a process I'm still engaged in today.

CM: Name some of the projects you have worked on, what was your involvement, what did you enjoy and what did you hate?

Brett: I've been making movies for thirty something years so there were a lot of projects. Most of them I've produced, written and directed myself, although occasionally I worked on other people's movies, like Don Farmer's *Body Shop/Deady Memories* and more recently Greg Lamberson's *Killer Rack.* On the former I was hired as DP but was also there as a sort of directorial understudy, in case someone else had to jump and and direct the thing, which I actually did twice. On *Killer Rack* I just did effects, building both miniature and full sized tentacles and doing some stop morion. What did I enjoy and what did I hate? The shoots themselves, the principle photography are usually miserable, especially on my own movies. On other peoples' movies I'm not carrying the weight of the movie so it's usually a little less onerous, but it's still no fun. What did I enjoy? I think I'd have to do some serious thinking to answer that. Nothing immediately springs to mind. I always think of Norman Mailer's comment after he'd directed *Tough Guys Don't Dance:* "Making movies is hard work --- and I don't mean hard like writing a symphony, I mean hard like mining coal."

CM: What kind of budgets do you generally work with and what kind of time constraints?

Brett: Very, very small budgets. The biggest budget I ever had on a movie was around $140,000 for *Shock-O-Rama,* alhtough some of that was wasted. The smallest I won't reveal. You wouldn't believe me. Generally I shoot a week or two, and then spend months to years doing the post, editing and shooting effects. My latest feature, *Outpost Earth,* took two years to complete, most of it doing effects.

CM: What is you favorite part of the movie making process?

Brett: Usually pre-production. Writing used to be fun and easy but lately it's becoming a chore. Maybe I'm running out of ideas. I like building the props and

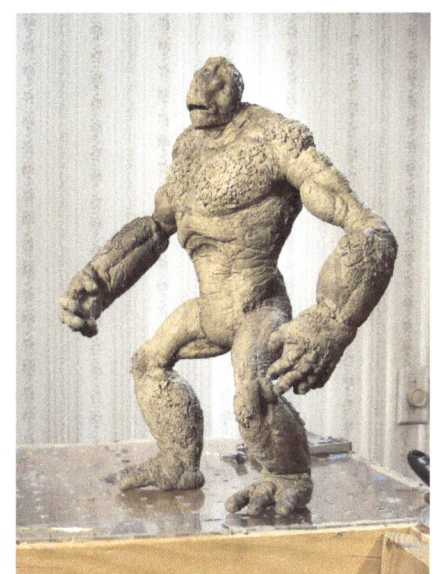

The Golum from Outpost Earth

monsters, and I like editing and seeing everything come togethger. I like the parts best where I'm left alone to work at my own pace. I hate deadlines, and racing against the clock.

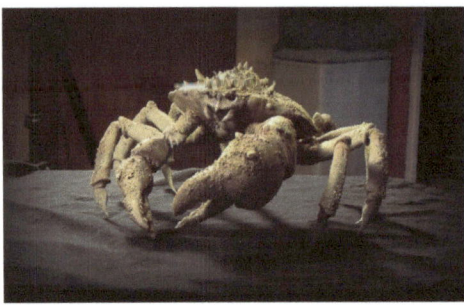

CM: How do you feel about CGI in the movies today?

Brett: Too much of it. Way, way, way too much. It's taken all the fun out of movies. It's supposed to enhance realism, but's instead it's made it impossible to believe anything you see. Nothing is impressive any more.

Queen Crab

CM: What are you currently working on?

Brett: I've been making short movies based on classic novels. I did *First Men in the Moon*

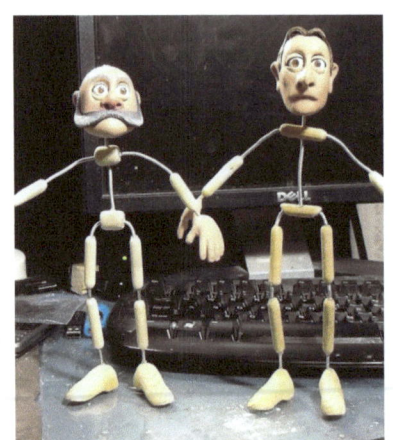
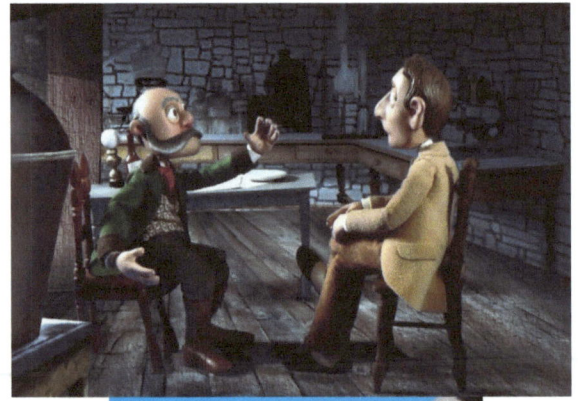
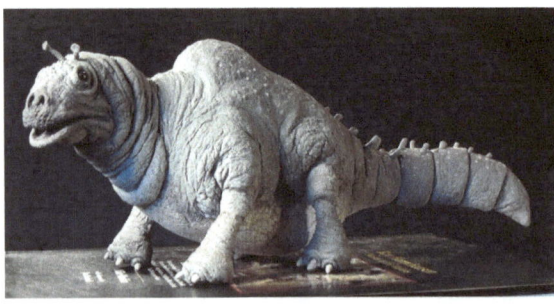
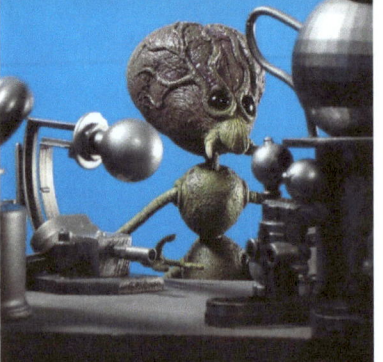

Characters and creatures from the stop-motion First Men in the Moon

and now I'm working on *20,000 Leagues Under the Sea.*

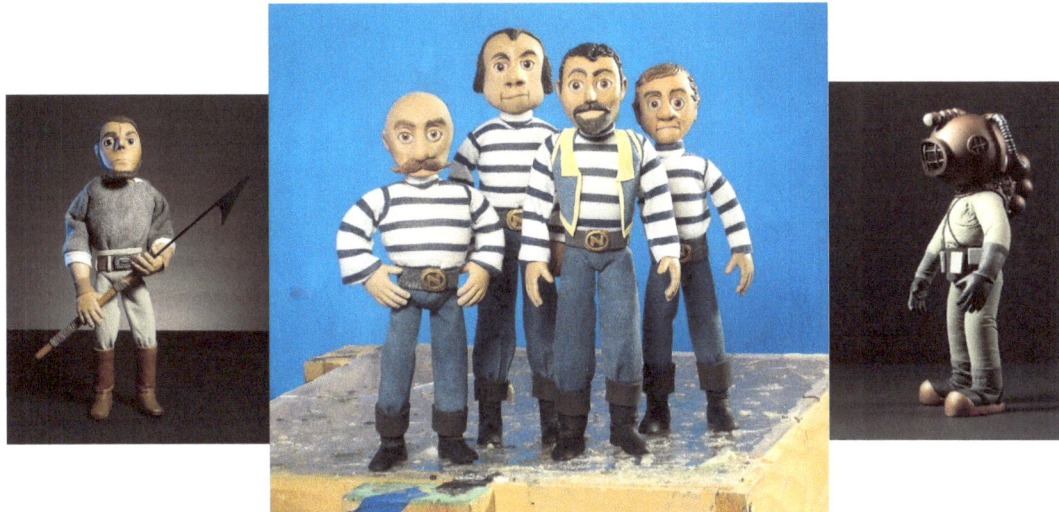

20,000 Leagues Under the Sea stop-motion characters

I may shoot another feature in the spring. It depends on if I can cast it. There's not much of a talent pool around here to speak of, and I don't have the money to bring people in.

CM: Do you have any how-to advice for people just starting out with little resources?

Brett: It's cheaper and easier than ever to make a low budget movie. But it's getting damn near impossible to sell them!

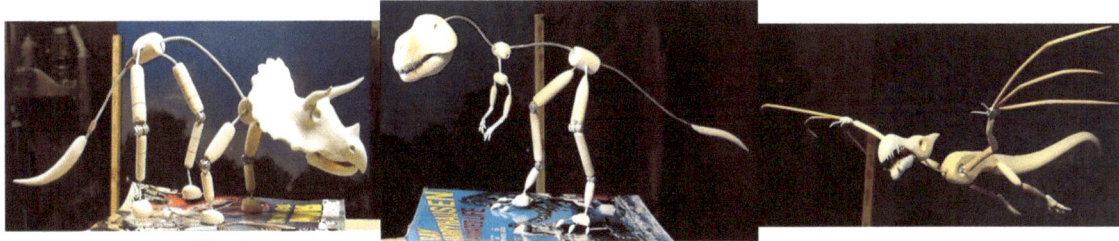

In progress dinosaur armatures for unidentified project

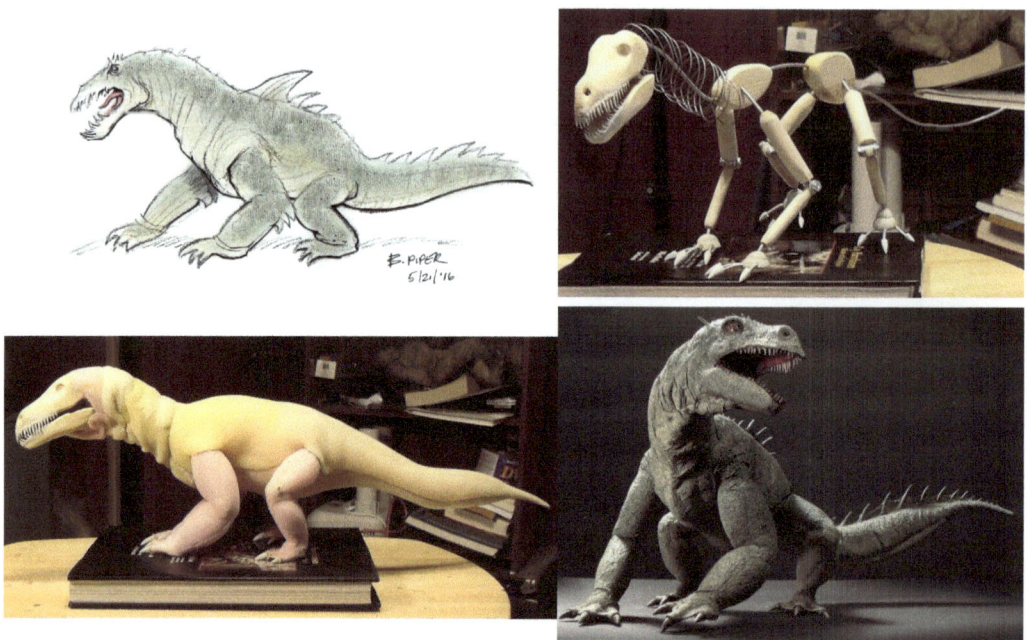

Process of building a creature

CM: Visit Brett on Amazon.com at: **https://tinyurl.com/y7lfggdf** and show him some love with a movie purchase.

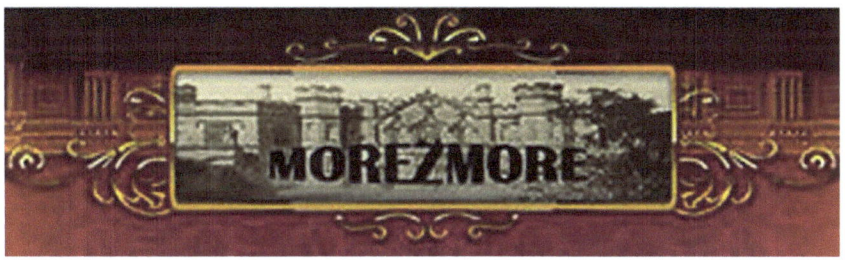

Morezmore Humanly Posable Armature (HPA)

by Natasha Nazaroza

HPA is a metal parts system to construct a strong lightweight dynamic humanoid skeleton for articulated puppets and dolls.

"Wow, awesome doll. Does she move?"
"She looks alive…She looks like she is about to take a step".

This is what I heard from people who saw Miss Marple – a 1:6 art doll. But Miss Marple could not walk or move, she was a statue, permanently frozen in one place, in one pose.

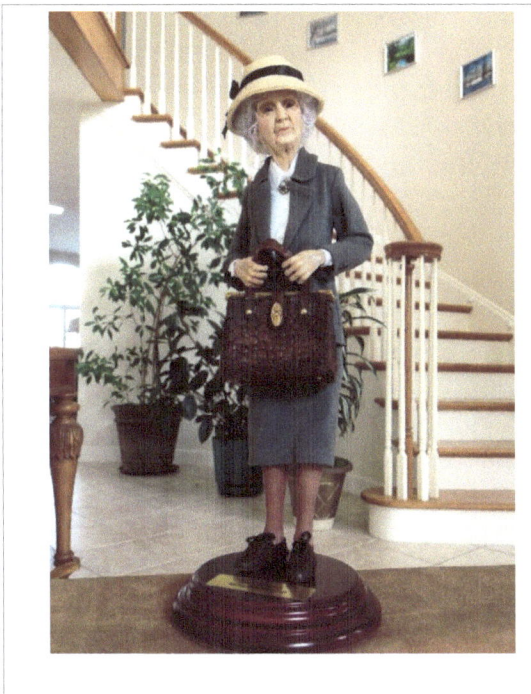
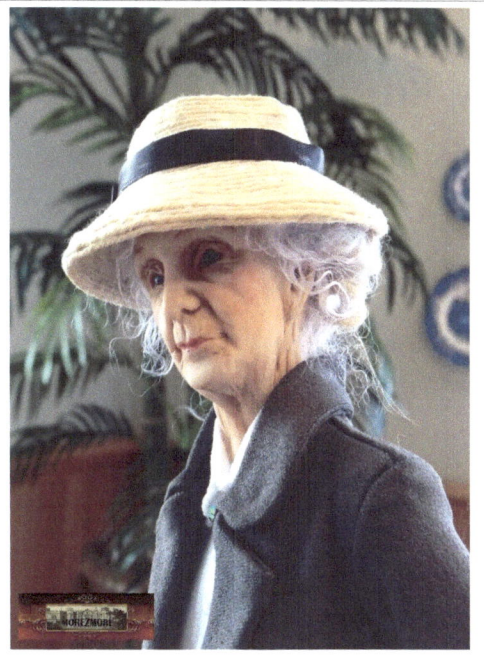

Step-by-step blog:
https://morezmore.wordpress.com/category/33-miss-marple/

So I decided to make my dolls move. It is not that this idea never crossed my mind before – in the past I made dolls with posable wire armatures and even tried Asian ball-jointed doll style construction. But those two ways had their limitations and I lost interest. This time I decided to use a ball and socket metal armature – the type that is used for stop motion puppets.

As I discovered, in order to get such an armature, an artist had two options:

1. Buy a pre-fabricated stop-motion armature from a professional. These stop-motion armatures are wonderful. They are made by professional artists craftsmen which use metal-cutting, tooling and machining equipment. The result is fantastic. The price is… fair if you keep in mind that the project involves a skillful metalwork craftsman with expensive power tools working many hours.

2. Make it from scratch. This option is certainly in the tradition of One of a Kind Art Dolls, as OOAK artists make everything themselves – from armature to accessories. But that would mean one has to BECOME a skillful metalwork craftsman with expensive power tools. And be prepared for cutting, drilling, milling, grinding and soldering metal. Not to mention buying the power equipment and setting the machine shop in the basement, complete with ventilation and noise-insulation systems.

As I did not see myself going into this kind of trouble, I wanted to find a third option – a construction set, something like a set for building a truck or helicopter, but for an articulated humanoid figure. A set of standardized inter-connecting pieces that would allow for the construction of a variety of different models and sizes. A set that would avoid the lead-time of designing complex systems and manufacturing custom pieces. A set that would not require special training to assemble. A set that would be affordable for a hobby artist. I did not find such set. If you cannot find it, make it.

This idea became an obsession project for the following year which I spent thinking about this cross-industry project, looking for standard steel parts all over the internet, figuring out shapes and sizes from photos, converting metrics millimeters to US inches and back, talking to vendors and manufacturers in different countries, buying parts, waiting for long international deliveries, trying to fit the parts together, getting alternatively excited and discouraged. The project was promising enough to keep me going – almost there, almost works, one more thing to figure out. I stuck with it.

I finally got all the parts together for a workable set and made Monsieur Poirot, as an experiment.

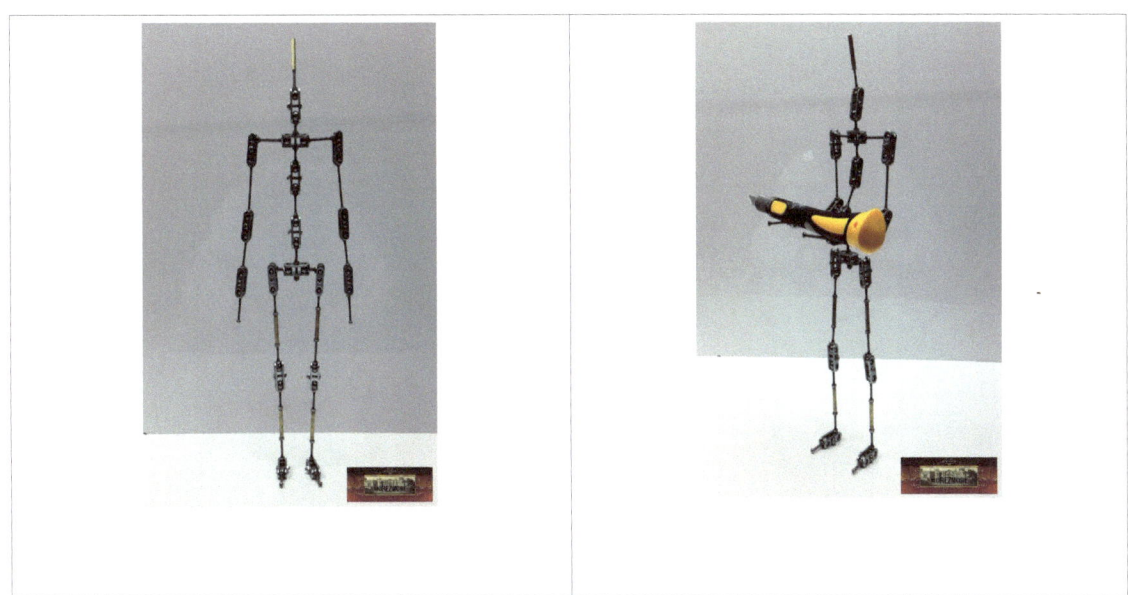

Poirot Blog Post: https://morezmore.wordpress.com/category/34-poirot/

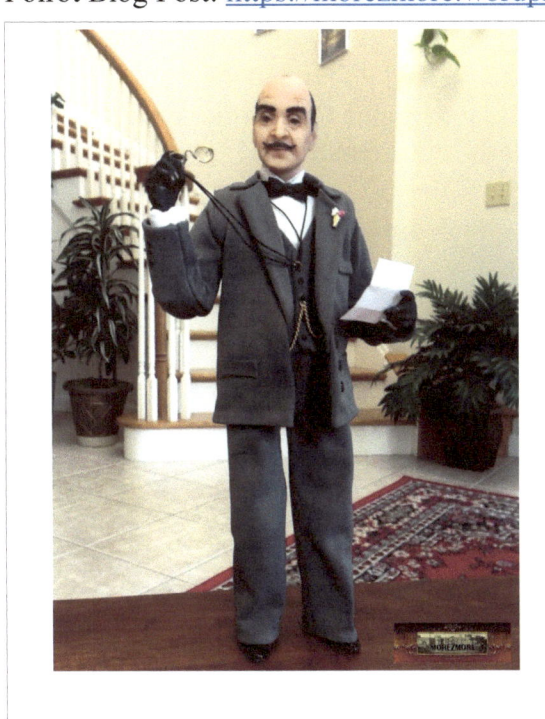
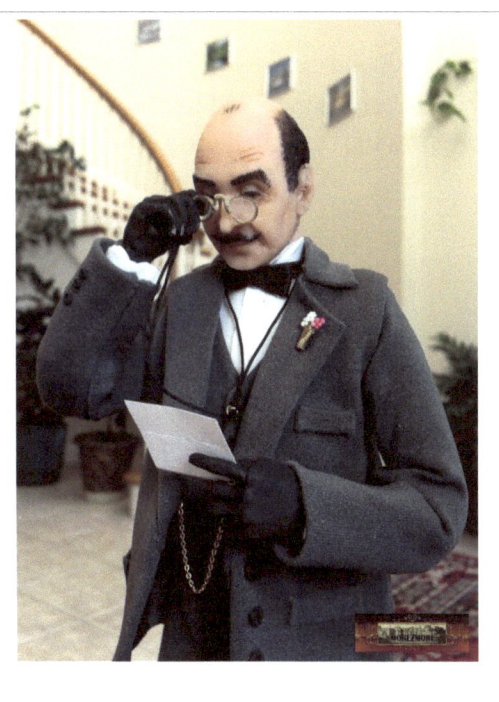

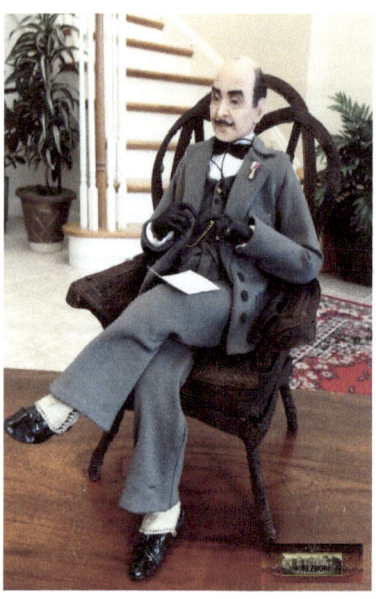 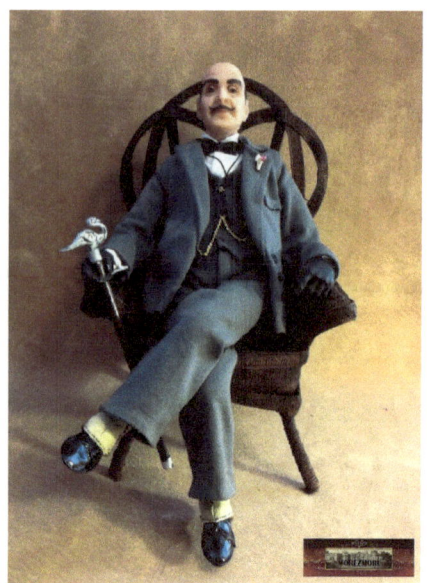

The response was fantastic. Folks on Facebook really liked Poirot and the whole idea. Inspired, I continued and made several more dolls, at the same time working on improving the design and figuring out how to "flesh" the armature.

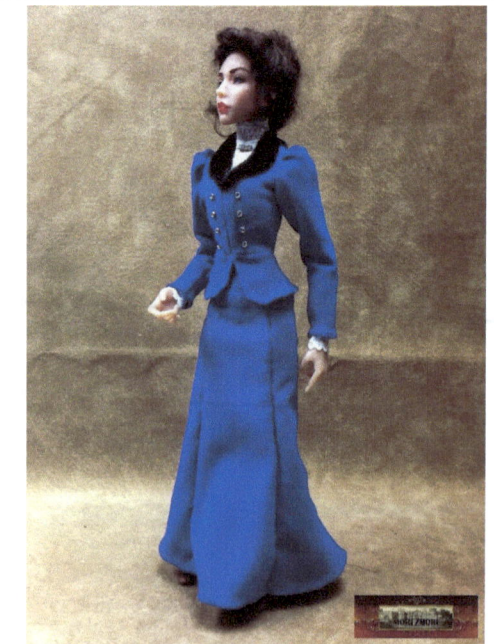

Anna Blog post:
https://morezmore.wordpress.com/category/35-anna-humanly-posable-doll/

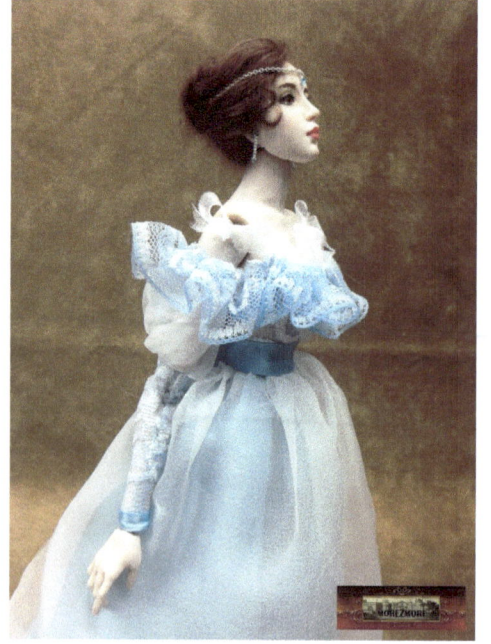

Nathalie Blog post:
https://morezmore.wordpress.com/2017/07/14/morezmore-natalie-humanly-posable-doll/

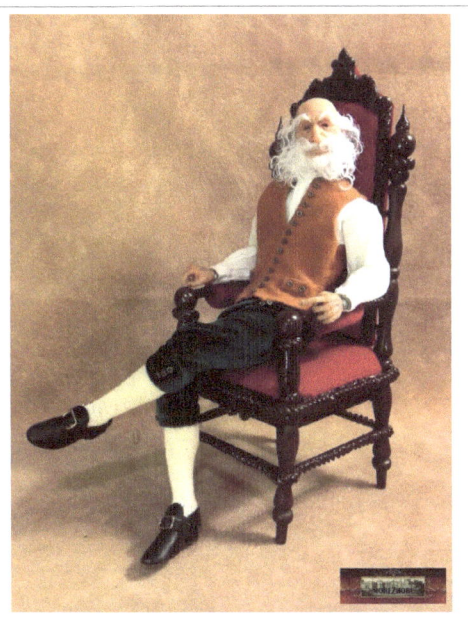 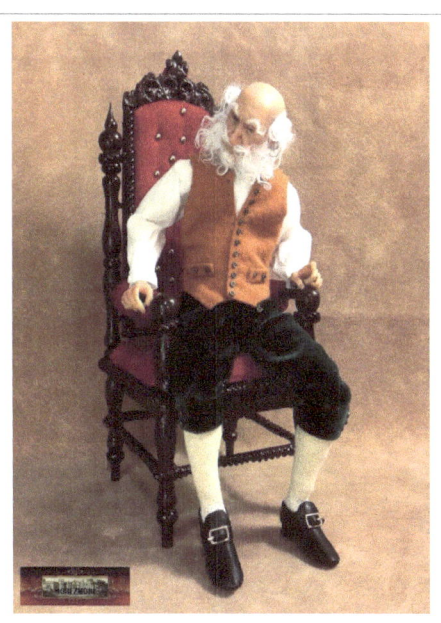

Historian Blog post:
https://morezmore.wordpress.com/category/37-historian/

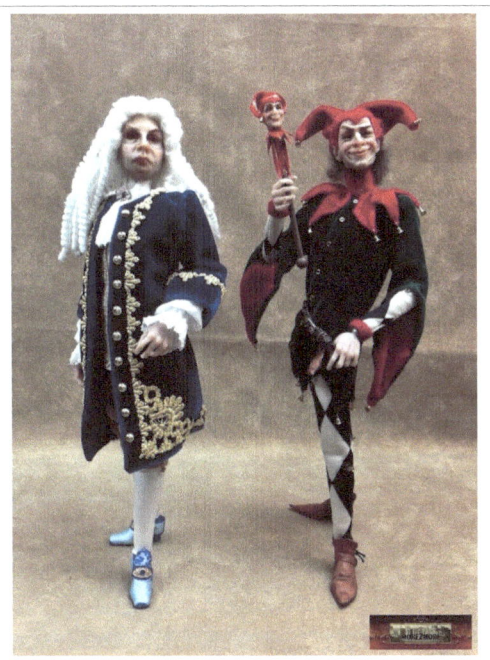 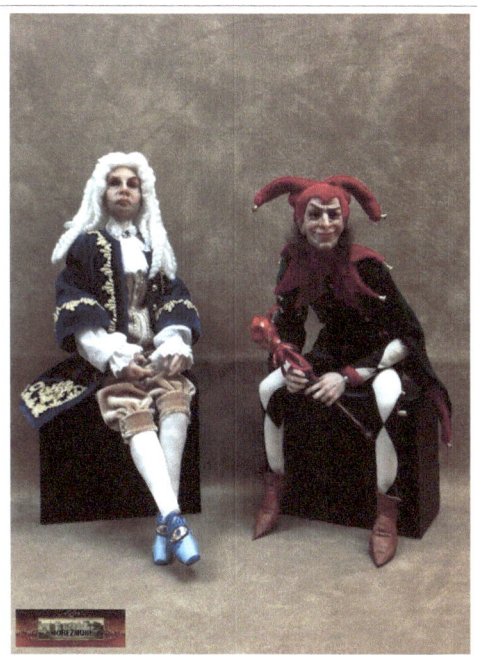

King and Jester Blog Post:
https://morezmore.wordpress.com/category/38-king-and-jester/

Finally, I got all parts together, made kits and called it the system Humanly Posable Armature (a play on words "humanly possible") The kits, as well as all individual parts, are available for purchase.

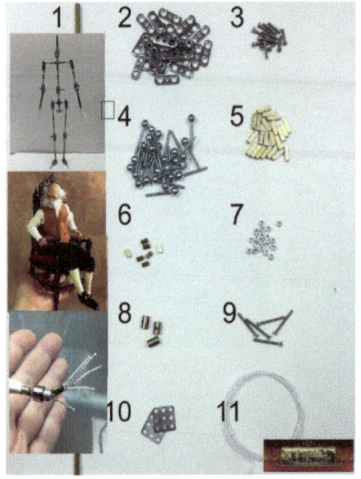

To summarize, HPA is an affordable system of inter-connecting parts, which allows for the construction of a dynamic humanoid skeleton in 1:6 scale (about 11-12" or 27-30 cm). Other sizes are possible, but not tested yet. Some of HPA parts are standard hardware, and some of them I had to order custom. The system offers a magnetic wrist joint option, which allows to pose the hands in any humanly possible way and even have several sets of hands made in different positions and replace them on the fly as needed for the photo.

HPA is still developing:
HPA-1-Basic - available for purchase
HPA-1-Basic with Magnetic Wrist Joints - available for purchase
HPA-2-Improved - will be available end of December, 2017
HPA-3-Superflex - final stages of the development, available beginning of January, 2018.

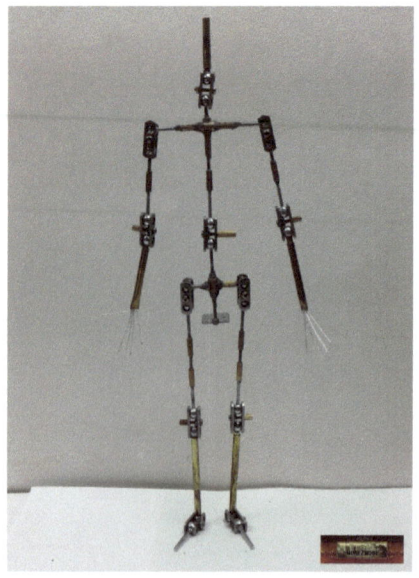

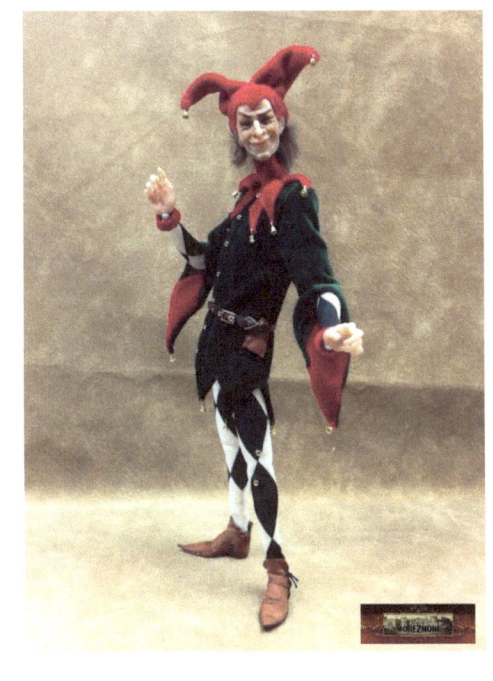 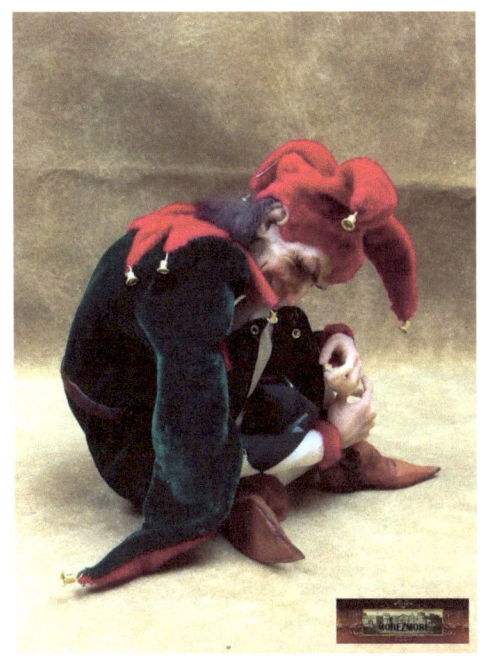

The latest puppet - Jester - has the HPA-3-Superflex armature, he is very lithe and graceful, able to assume more poses than the puppets with HPA Basic. Jester can even roll into a ball.

The instructions for how to put parts and kits together can be found on Morezmore blog: https://morezmore.wordpress.com/. The links to purchase the kits are also there.
The blog has a lot of information on how to "flesh" the skeleton, dress the puppet and make accessories and furniture.

There is a Facebook discussion group "Humanly Posable Armature Sandbox", it is public and everybody is welcome to join:

https://www.facebook.com/groups/163386914241632/

I will be interested to see other artists joining me on this project – using Humanly Posable Armature construction parts to create articulated art dolls and stop-motion puppets.

A Visit to the Zu-3D

Low budget stop-motion capture software

Review by

David A. D'Champ

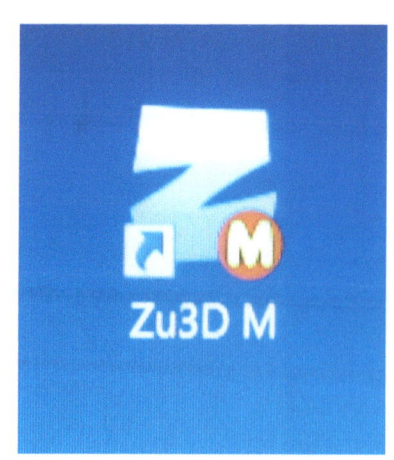

When I first started production of my latest mini-epic with my granddaughter, Charlotte, I knew I wanted to kick-up the quality of the FX we would be doing since we were also going to be going on location to film much of the project. I wanted the stop-motion integration into the live-action to be just a little bit better than what we had done for Escape from Skull Planet. So I started looking for the best stop-motion capture software that no money could buy. I knew I wanted it to have a live video channel for capture that could be chroma keyed over captured video. At first I thought about doing the stop-motion in front of a large video screen and just doing an overlay on the foreground to cover the animation table but that would have too many limitations for what I wanted to do. So I began an internet search.

After several days of search and only finding live chroma channel software for people like bloggers doing weather reports and absolutely nothing in the low cost, zero cost shareware/freeware varieties; I pretty much gave up. I knew higher end packages like Dragon and Eclipse had the features I wanted but my budget barely covered gas money to go to the local park we were going to film at. Then I found something in a final search called Zu3D. I had looked at this capture software before but this new version promised to do pretty much everything I wanted to do. It even had a trial version I could download that would give a month to test it. So, I downloaded and installed it and although it went through the effort, I could not get the live channel for the webcam to work so that I could 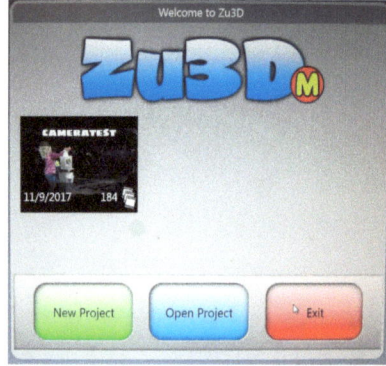 live-key stop-motion frame captures over my live-action footage. Disappointed I wrote to the company, ZuLogic and explained my problem with the software. To my surprise the company responded back in less than a day and wanted to set up a live, interactive trouble shooting session to try and figure out why the software wasn't working. After about three hours of online tweaking and a little cursing the problem was found and solved. To my amazement, because of my willingness to work with them, I was given a free license to the software.

And I was off.

I've always been a little off but this software really set me off. To be honest I was never really thrilled with the interface design but to be fair it is aimed at kids and the education market so who am I to criticize. Using it I feel there needs to be a more adult/Pro version and I was happy to learn that the company shares my feelings and has plans for a more professional interface with more advanced features.

But for now the loading screen allows you access to all that there is to this magical software package.

While the software is full featured with a timeline that an entire movie could be produced on, it is severely limited in that arena and I only planned on using if for stop-motion capture and compositing with the chroma feature.

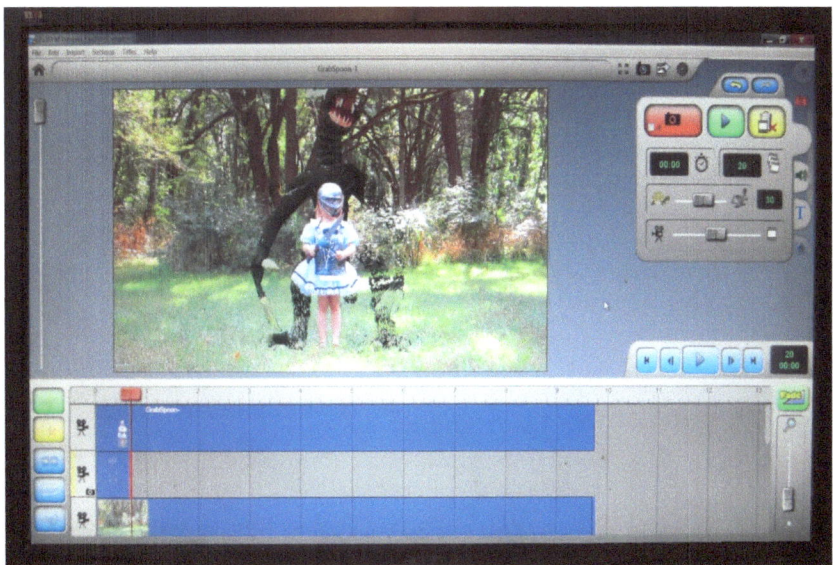

Above is a picture of the basic program layout. As you can see in the timeline the images is a layer of live-action at the top with background keyed and painted out with a layer of stop-motion capture directly below that with it's background keyed out. And finally a static photo background to complete the image to easily create what should be a very difficult shot of having the stop-motion behind the live-action. The interface is a colorful, overly clunky design that is obviously for kids but offers exceptional bang for the buck. While the bottom timeline is where all the media resides, the magick happens in the upper right hand corner of the screen.

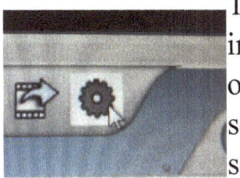
This little gear shaped widget is for opening the programs settings interface. You can also access the setting from the drop down menu on the upper left side of the screen. It is important to go to these setting each time the program is used as the program doesn't save settings between uses. Also, on problematic computers like mine, if

you don't tweak the settings the program could possibly freeze or crash. This is not to say this is a twitchy program, its not, it is a very stable program and generally functions flawlessly. My computer is twitchy. So click on the gear and let's look under the hood.

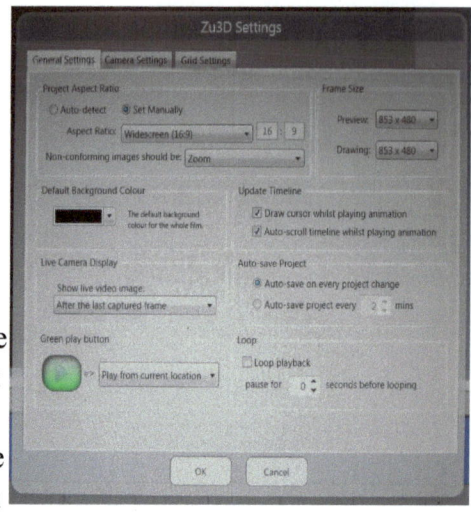

The settings dialog has three panels that cover the General Settings, Camera Settings, and Grid Settings. In the Camera Setting you can select between No Camera, Web Camera, and a Remote Camera. A remote camera is a cellphone with a built in camera that has the Zu3D App loaded. This only works if your computer network has WiFi active. The Web camera setting is probably the most commonly used. I've noted that if you are using a webcam with an extension USB cable that there can be connect detection problems that can cause the software to freeze so try to used only the cable connection with the webcam or possibly run the camera through a powered hub to increase cable distance. You also need to set the camera frame refresh rate at around 10fps. Faster speeds can cause problems depending on your setup.

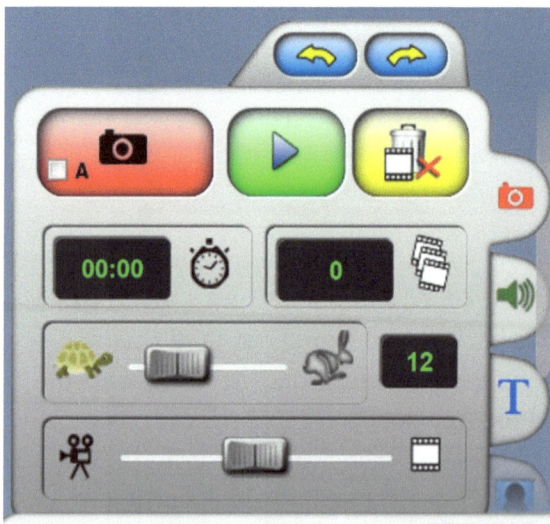

This is the main tool box found on the top right of the program screen. The bent yellow arrows are Undo/Redo. The Red button with a camera is the capture button. The Green button will play the clip. The Yellow button with the frame, X and trash can removes the currently highlighted frame on the timeline. The counter with the clock is the current time/frame location on the timeline and next to that is the current frame number. The turtle to rabbit slider can be used to set the FPS and camera to frame slider sets the onionskin level where the camera is the live video feed and the frame is the last frame captured. Somewhere in the middle is the best level of blending to see where you were and where you are going.

The bottom icon on the far right slider bar of the tool box access the Green Screen Tool box. A click of the green button attempts to grab and key the closest color to green found in the video clip or the live webcam feed to key out a green background behind a stop-motion puppet. This grab is usually pretty close but if there are shadows, hot spots or other background color problems you will end up with some color static on the background. The captured color will have a slider you can use to try and clean up the edges but you can also select a second key color if needed. 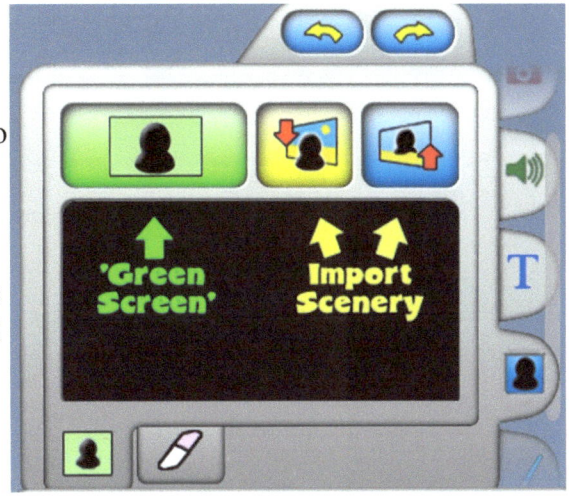 In fact you can select as many colors as you want and each will have a slider adjustment. But this method is messy at best and tends to create more problems than it solves. If you look at the bottom of the tool box you find a tab with what looks like a white/pink eraser. Click this to be amazed.

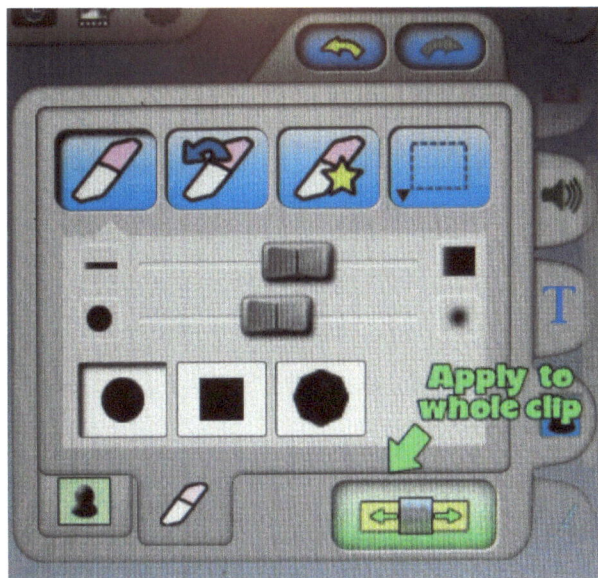 The first eraser allows you to erase any problem on the screen that is messing up the chroma. The second eraser allows you to 'fix' something removed by the chroma and get it back into the shot. The starred eraser allows you to copy a previous frame as a background behind the current frame to use as a 'fix' when erasing parts of an image. The final shape select allows you select, copy, cut, erase or manipulate a portion of a frame in various ways. The sliders on the first three tools allow you to change the size of the selected shape and how much edge feathering it has. Finally, the "Apply to whole clip" button does just that. It applies the finished edits to the entire clip to give you a quick starting point to do finish editing for each frame of a clip if needed.

In my humble opinion I find this green screen application and cleanup tools to be some of the finest available on any level in the video industry. And, on top of that, they are SO easy to use.

I will use a clip from my mini-epic. The Lost Forest as an example of using the green screen cleanup tools.

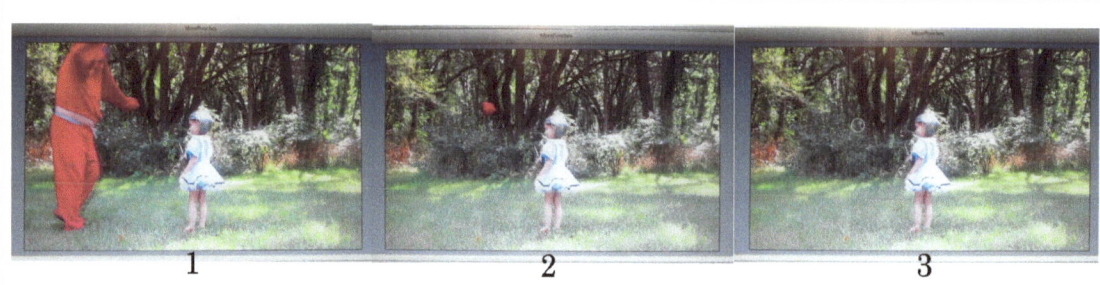

1	2	3
Frame one is me with my granddaughter playing out the attack of the Jabberwock.	Using the selection tool I erased most of myself from the frame so that a static background image could show through.	Finally, using the eraser tool I cleaned up the image to remove the last portion of me from the frame.

The finished frame shows Charlotte fighting with the Jabberwock instead of her PopPop. The software allows for very close interaction between the live-action and the stop-motion and brings to mind the process Ray Harryhausen called Dynamation and Dynarama. With very little work and practice by the animator, many very amazing things can be accomplished with Zu-3D. Although this is a huge iceberg for many stop-motion artists, it is still just the tip of the program.

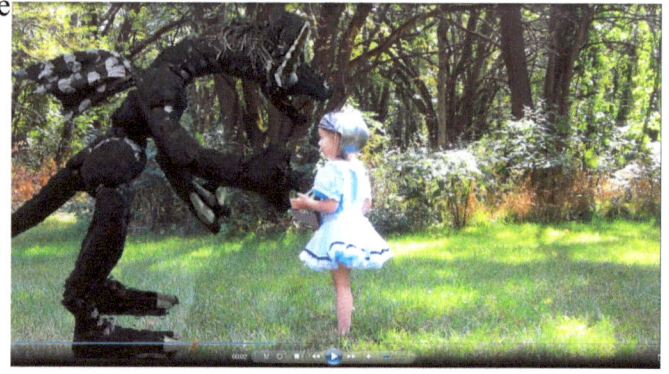

The program allows for layering sounds onto a clip and even has a titling program. In truth a full video could be produced using this software but don't throw away your standalone video editing program yet. Unless you are using that POS made by Microsoft.

The program has some quirks and some of it's methods of storing data are a bit wasteful of hard drive space but the programmers reasoning for these are acceptable. Be prepared to gobble up gigabytes if you use this program for anything larger than a project of a few minutes. If you dream of doing the next Sinbad feature, invest in a terabyte drive to make it. The highest resolution the program saves to is 1920x1080 for full HD video in the MP4 format. I'm hoping the pro version will allow even higher resolution to allow users to do full Blu-ray and potentially 4K productions.

Every program has it's pros and cons. This program was written for easy of use for kids and that shows. But the quality of what this program can do for the low budget stop-motion movie maker far out weights any and all cons the program might have. Dollar for dollar Zu3D is a gold mine compared to any of the other software out there including Dragonframe. The customer service alone is worth the price of the program.

Give ZuLogic a visit https://zu3d.com/ and give the program a trial run and decide for yourself.

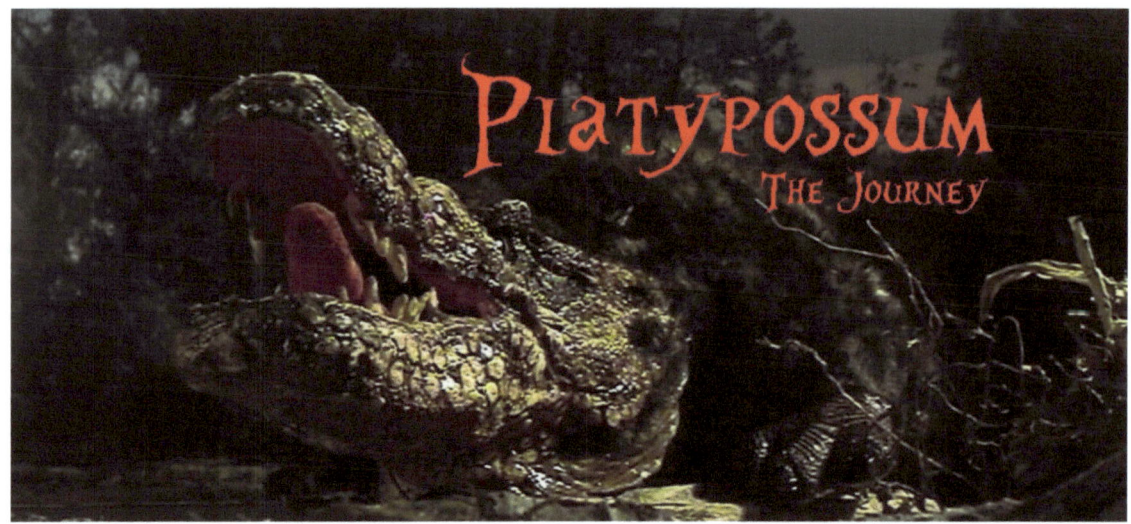

PLATYPOSSUM – The Journey

By

Roger Dale Trexler

Writer/Director of PLATYPOSSUM – THE MOVIE

© 2017 Roger Dale Trexler

When I was first stricken with the sickness that made me think I could make a low budget feature film, I went about writing the script. Common sense told me to use locations I knew. But, not having a lot of common sense, I decided that I would make a stop motion animation film. Not only that, but a stop motion film about a *mutated* monster ala those wonderful Saturday afternoon monster movies of my youth.

Over drinks one evening, I talked to my partner in crime, artist Brad Moore, and he assured me he could design a creature for a stop motion film.

So, I set about writing the script. I knew pretty early on that I wanted to made a throwback to the science fiction films of my youth, where the creature was created by mankind's foolishness. But, unlike those Saturday afternoon films where creatures were created from radiation, I decided on a timelier topic: hydraulic fracturing. They'd been trying to frack the Shawnee National Forest in southern Illinois for several years at the time—and a license was granted recently, then rescinded—and that topic is a divisive subject. So, I came up with the idea that the evil corporation was testing a new fracking compound that had mutating properties…. thereby creating the Platypossum.

I won't go into details about how a platypus comes to southern Illinois and escapes, gets coit with a possum and creates a monster…. you'll have to see the movie for that. It should be available for download via Amazon in December 2017.

Instead, I will detail the production of the film.

Ok. The first thing you need when creating a stop motion creature is the idea for what the creature will look like. Brad Moore did the design work. He spent a lot of time drawing out how the creature should appear. What would the mutant offspring of a platypus and a possum look like? Certainly, not much like either creature. The limitations of budget (which was practically nonexistent—we had the desire, but not the cash) created its own set of problems. Brad created the large "bust" of the monster head from something that I am sworn to secrecy about—and I will not reveal it here. If you want to know what the original large creature head was made of, you'll have to send me copious amounts of cash. Suffice it to say, you'll laugh your ass off….and the solution is/was brilliantly redneck in its executions.

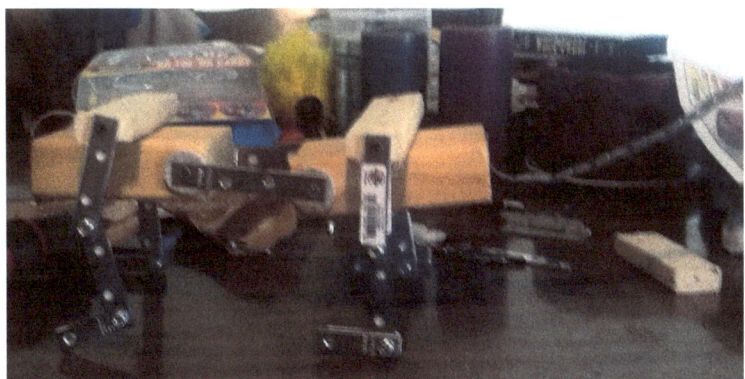

But, I digress.

We used the creature head several times in the finished film, but we need a real "live" creature to made the movie possible. Brad was teaching school and did not have the time to create the armature for the creature, so the task fell on me.

Now, once again, the budget came to bear. We did not have the money to creature a perfectly machined armature. That would have cost thousands (even in Harryhausen's day they cost an arm and a leg). So, I set out to create an armature on a nonexistent budget.

I pondered on the problem for weeks. I tried creating an all wire armature, but that just seemed too flimsy for what we were attempting. So, in the end, I took a 2x4 piece of wood and cut off a couple pieces. From there, I went to the hardware store and bought some metal strap pieces, some nuts and bolts and washers, and a few wood screws. I put the armature together in about an hour and the final cost of all parts was probably in the neighborhood of twenty dollars.

From there, we had to put the skin and head on the monster.

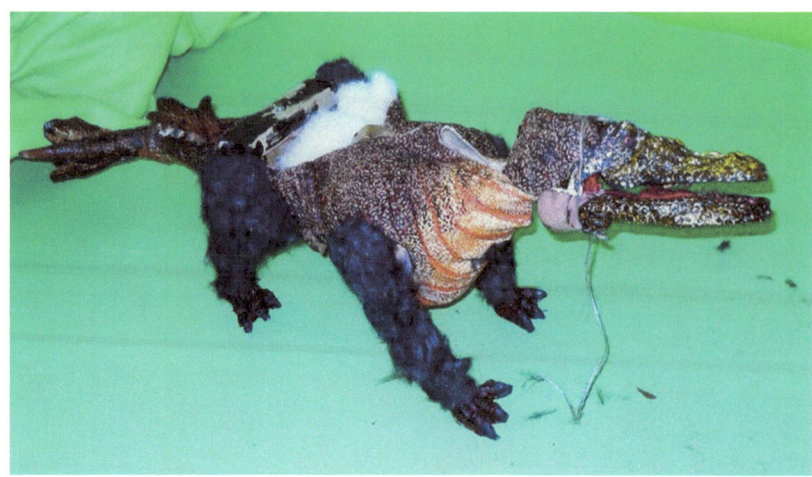

Brad Moore's brother, Wade, of Brainstorms Laboratories, did the molding of the head and feet and scales. A quick trip to the local fabric shop provided the fur necessary to create our hairy monster. We attached the head to the armature through a couple wood screws and a very thick piece of bendable wire (so the head could bend, of course). The tail was really just a scaly piece of skin wrapped around toy stuffing and another piece of that thick wire. We overlooked filing down the end of the wire and/or bending back in on itself and, several times during production, had to fix a hole at the end of the tail where the wire poked through.

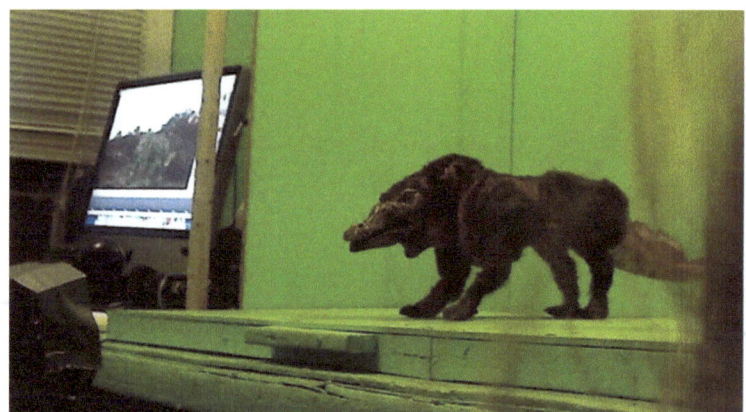

Finally, we had a monster we could film.

We took a piece of pegboard, put a "foundation" around it so we could work, and started animating. The wire clips Brad used in the beginning presented a problem (if you showed the feet, you showed the wire clips), so I devised a way of attaching the monster to the pegboard through the bottom of the pegboard. I took the original molds Wade Moore had done and created a wire frame for the feet (which also meant that they could "clamp" the toes) and set a threaded "boot" inside the feet. Once the feet had molded, I attached them to the monster, took some wing-nutted screws and attached the creature to the pegboard table.

It worked fairly well. Not brag-worthy, but at least you didn't see the wires anymore.

Another problem with the original armature were the legs. They just didn't have the bendability we needed. So, they had to go. I came up with the idea of using electrical wire and pvc pipe in the legs. I attached them and, for the most part, the animation you see in the final film was done with those legs.

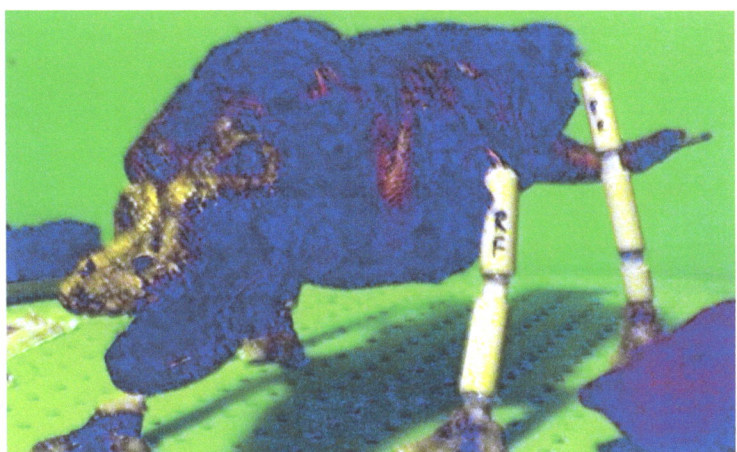

There were other problems, of course. The creature liked to lean to one side a lot, so it was a constant battle to keep it level. The latex, when it dried, was quite brittle and had to be redone several times throughout production.

And walking. Walking was a pain in the arse. But, a monster that can not walk isn't much of a monster. I pondered on how to make the creature walk in a realistic manner for quite some time. In the end, I came up with a "track and rut" set up that worked…. sort of. I did no less than a dozen test runs of the set up before I achieved a useable take for the film. If you're making an animal walk, I highly recommend going online and finding a diagram of how an animal actually walks. I think the diagram I found was that of a cat walking.

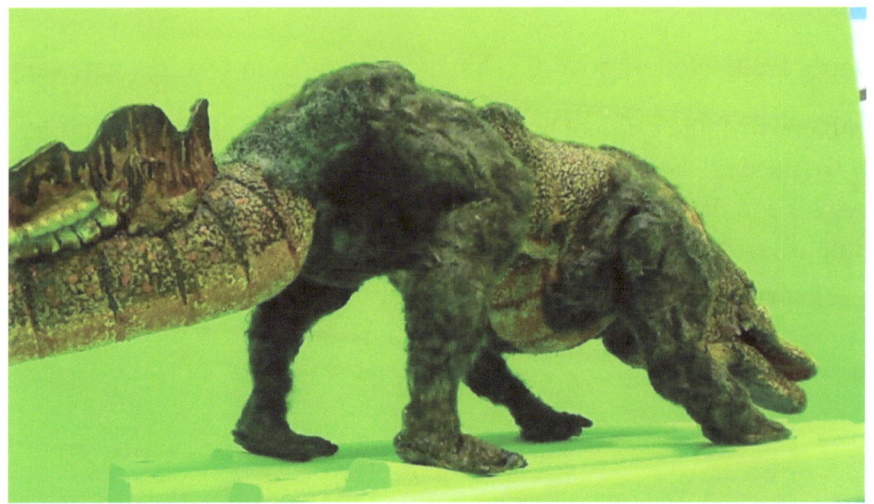

Other problems included: the creature rearing into the air, eating an unsuspecting news reporter, eating a priest giving baptisms and a girl out hiking. We created miniature versions of those people out of small imposable dolls, and stuck them in the mouth of the creature and animated it. Those scenes are some of my favorite scenes in the movie.

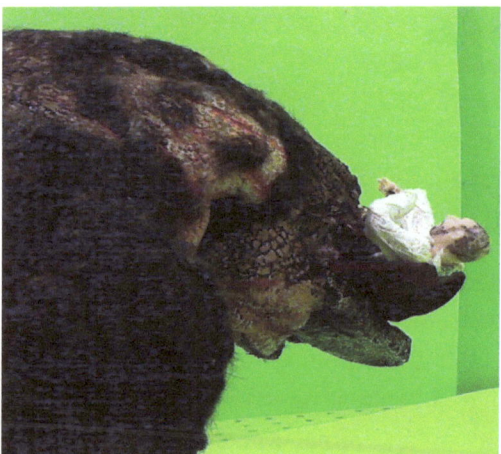

With the climatic scene, I needed a hydraulic fracking tower. I built two of them. One was solid and the other one was collapsible. Some sound effects and special effects make that seem fairly effective, too.

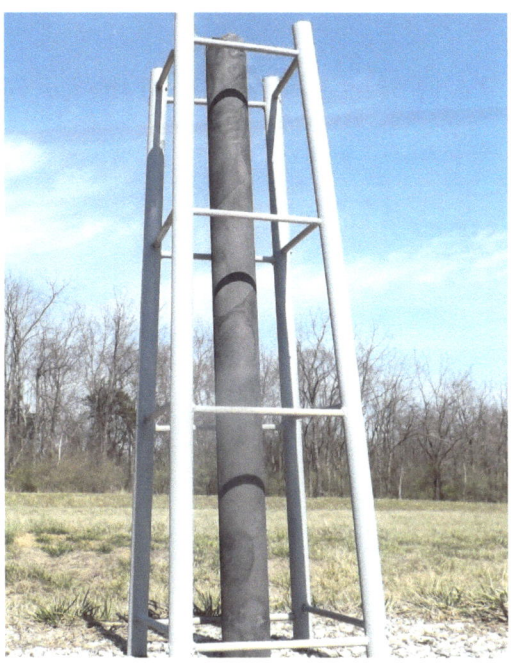

In the end, PLATYPOSSUM-THE MOVIE was thousands of hours of work. There were times when I became overwhelmed and thought about giving up. But, thankfully, I'm a stubborn man and I seldom take "no" for an answer.

The film got finished and premiere locally on August 18, 2017. It has shown a few times over the ensuing months, and I am now actively seeking a distributor to unleash this low-budget stop motion monster flick upon the world.

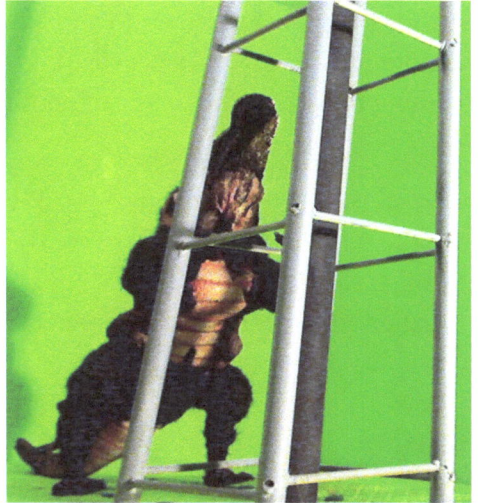

I learned a lot during the making of this film (I even taught myself After Effects to clean up the green screens I used on all of the animation – the lighting was wrong and the creature was green) and I will be doing another stop motion film in the not too distant future. That movie will be an adventure, too; but like a first born child, PLATYPOSSUM-THE MOVIE will always hold a special place in my heart.

The Lost Forest/Last Voyage of the Lovecraft

A Lewis Carroll Adventure meets HP Lovecraft

by David D'Champ

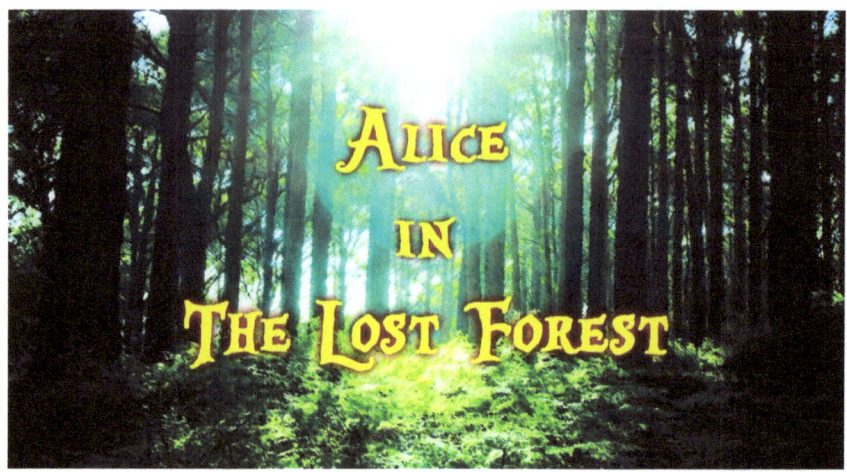

Mimsy were the Borogove. But no one said hunting the Jabberwock would be easy.

Where do stories likes the adventures of Alice in Wonderland come from? Many times from the children themselves.

I was watering the lawn one day with the help of my granddaughter, Charlotte, and as we were putting the hose away she announced she wanted to explore the Lost Forest. I asked her what she meant by that and she said she wanted to do an Alice adventure. Now we had already done several adventure movies together because she loves stop-motion but she had never mentioned something involving the works of another writer other than her PopPop. I was intrigued.

So while she spent the afternoon on the swing set we discussed what she wanted the story to be about and in short order we had outlined the basic idea of The Lost Forest adventure. Adapting the poem about the battle with the Jabberwock was easy to do and offered us a chance to go on location to a local forest reserve park to shoot most of the

movie. At the time we were also working on an idea for a TV show called Johnny Jupiter and together we decided this story would be an episode of our Johnny Jupiter series.

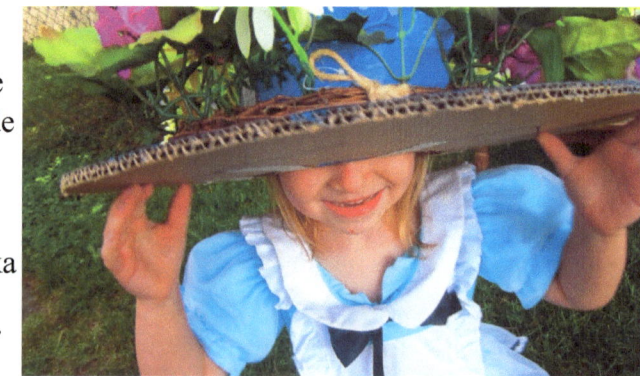

The live shoots went quickly with most of it happening at the Mishawaka Res, a state funded forest reserve and park. It was a massive undertaking of me and Charlotte wandering around the woods and stopping from time to time to shoot video of Charlotte meeting the various characters and talking with them. For the fight scene with the Jabberwock, we were joined by Grandma (Mawgah) so that she could work the camera while I stood in for the Jabberwock wearing all red so that I could 'easily' be removed from the green wooded background.

The Tea Party Massacre was staged in our back yard to allow a little more control over the shoot. Even some of the stop-motion of the conversation with the Dor-Mouse was done that same afternoon.

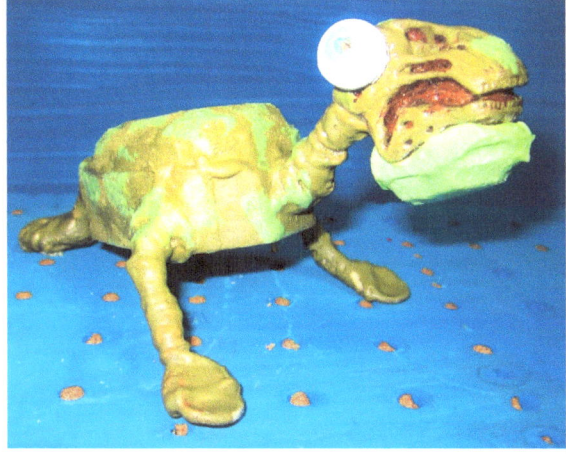

Slithy Tove

A total of 5 stop-motion puppets was planned for the production that would include the Slivey Toath, the Boragoves, the Dor-Mouse, Mome Rath and Jabberwock. Most all of the animation for the first four characters was complete and I was just starting on the Jabberwock when the bane of all computer users happened. A hard drive crash, And not just a minor crash, this one took out my 500gb main image storage drive. Being a low budget producer with no budget or cash flow this meant the movie was stalled until I could get a new hard drive. Luckily all of the complete segments had been transferred to another computer where the editing would be done but until I had a new hard drive I couldn't continue with the Alice production. Later I would discover that at least a half dozen walks in the woods with Charlotte had been lost and probably about two dozen background stills.

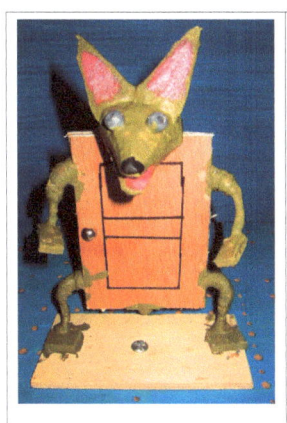

The Dor Mouse

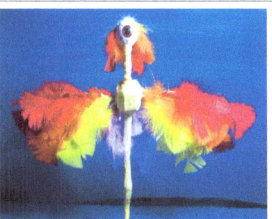

The Boragove

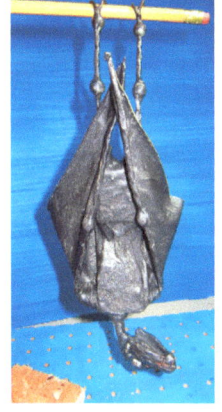

The Mome Rath

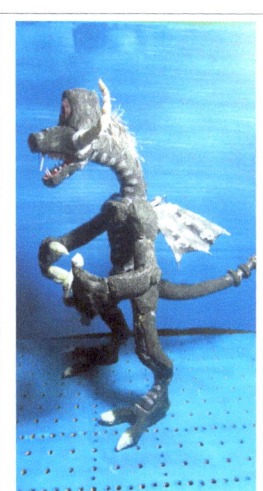

The Jabberwock

Since I had all the puppets for The Lost Forest completed, it felt like nothing was going to happen for a very long time. But my granddaughter doesn't work like that. One day shortly after the disaster Charlotte was playing with her collection of monster puppets from the other movies we had made and she asked me to show her pictures of new monsters. Recently I had been reading some HP Lovecraft so I decided to scare her with the Lovecraft mythology.

I failed to scare her.

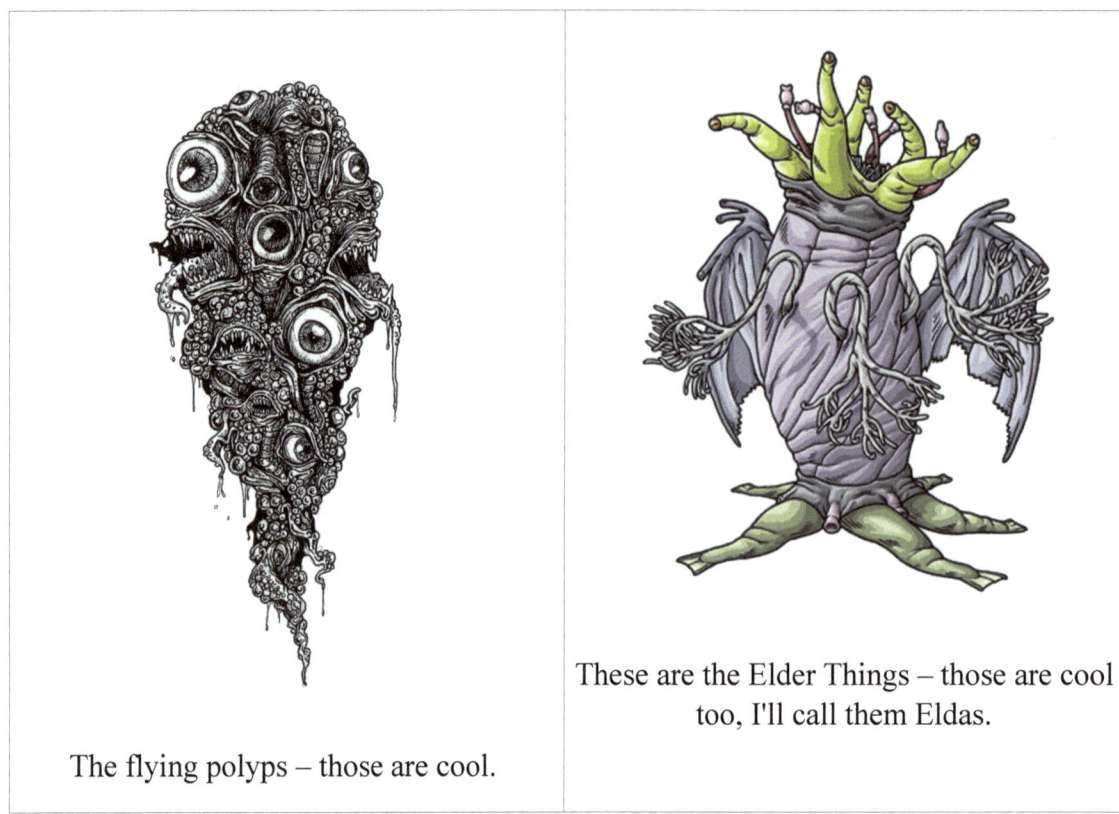

The flying polyps – those are cool.

These are the Elder Things – those are cool too, I'll call them Eldas.

Nothing seemed to phase her and the monsters just seemed to draw her further into the Lovecraft Mythos.

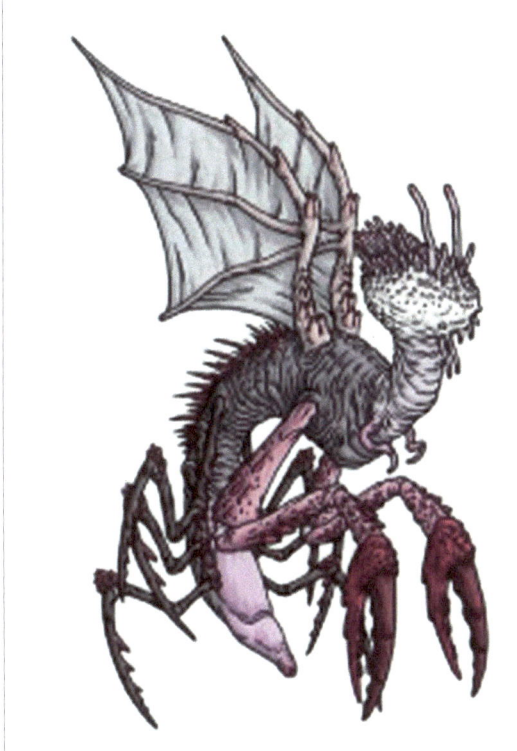

How about the Mi-Go – they look like hornets.

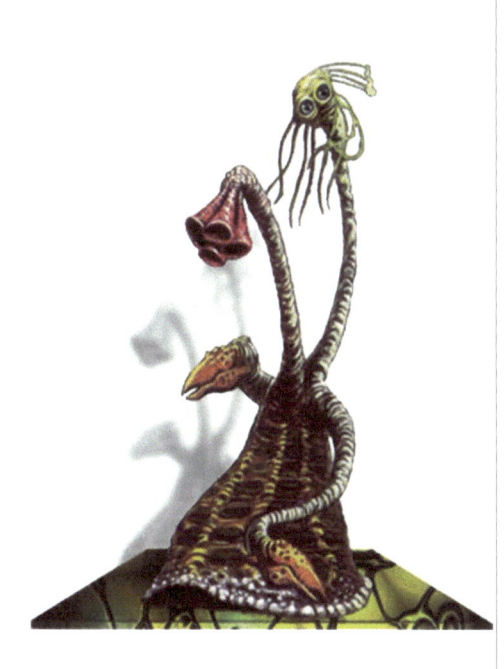

I really like the Yith.

What about Cthulhu? - Charlotte, "that's like my Hello Cthulhu doll. Can we do a Lovecraft movie? I want a river monster called an Elombah."

So I started my Q and A session with her throwing out story ideas and she's give them a thumbs up or a thumbs down. After a short while the basic of the story was that I would be an airship captain flying the Lovecraft and Charlotte would be my granddaughter over for a visit and we would end up in a world wide quest to find the city of R'lyeh and stopping Cthulhu, or maybe Cathulhu. Charlotte wanted her kitten to come along on the adventure with us.

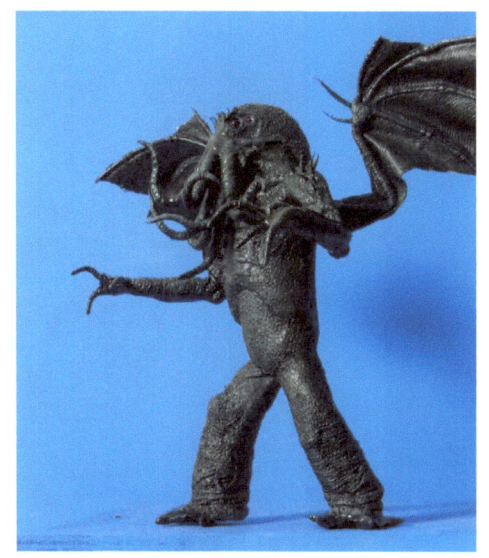

Cthulhu? I have one of those.

Well, by this time I had enough of a story seed to plant a tree. So I had something to do while waiting to get the new hard drive. That was enough to keep me busy but Charlotte still needed distraction. So while I worked on the script I started building stop-motion puppets of Lovecraft monsters for her to enjoy while hardware issues were worked on for The Lost Forest. I don't think I really had any plans to actually make the Lovecraft movie but it worked as a distraction for me. As I began to finish some of the stop-motion puppets for the Lovecraft story and as I got closer to finishing the script I began to realize this could be a really fun project. But it had evolved into a feature movie. Something Charlotte and I had not tried before.

So here I was with an almost completed Alice in Wonderland story, The Lost Forest, and an original Lovecraft story, The Last Voyage of the Lovecraft, with no money and no functional equipment to speak of.

But I did have supplies to build puppets and Charlotte loves the puppets.

So I continued building puppets because you do what you can when you can with what you have on hand.

The flying polyps became amorphous blobs of clay with eyes all over them and dug out gashes to form mouths. The Eldas had some sculpted body parts and a sculpted starfish head with a wire armature interior. The Yith ended up being a reworking of a puppet I had previously built Everything, the Elombah, Mi-Go and Cathulhu, was going to be a little more complex in terms of armature design. And then there would be the miniatures and scale models needed.

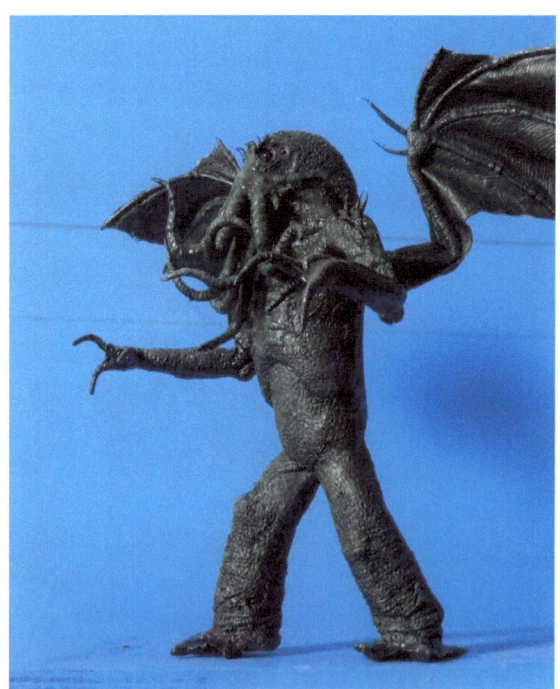

Cthulhu puppet by Richard Svenson

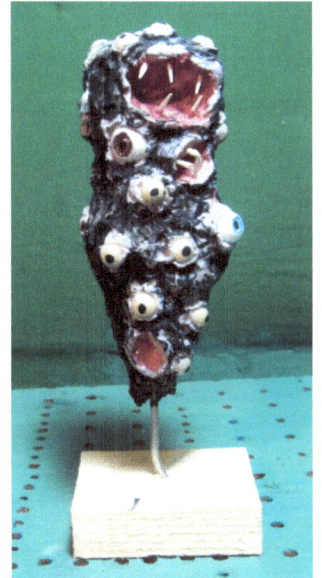

The Flying Polyp

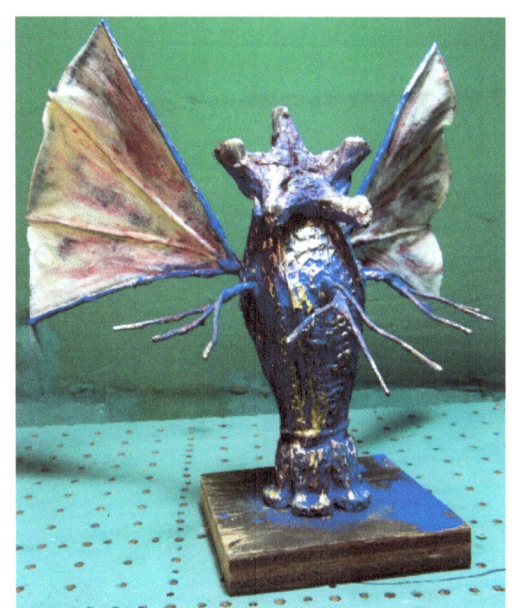

The Elder Thing (Elda)

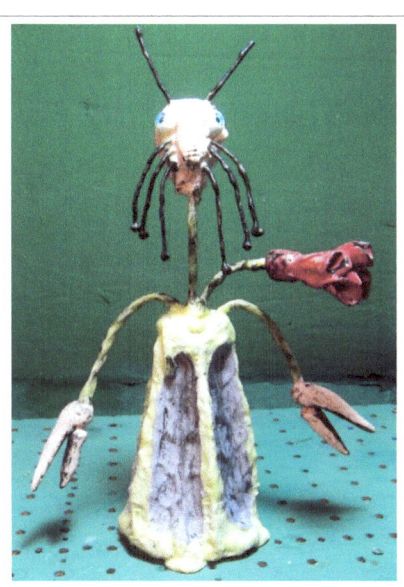

The Yith (Great Race)

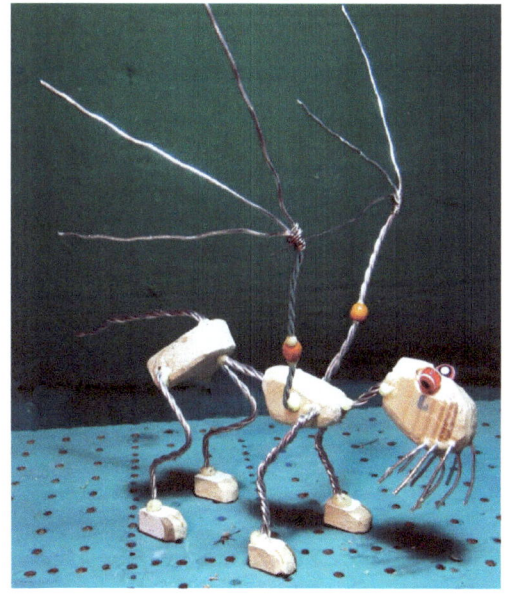

Cathulhu armature

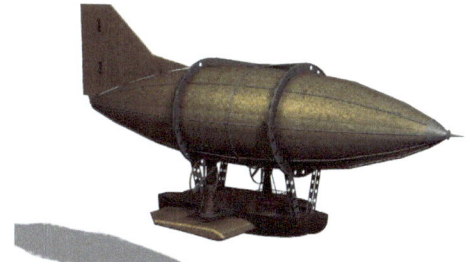

The airship Lovecraft

I wanted to get back to work on The Lost Forest and quick, and hope Charlotte would forget about Lovecraft. With the help of a friend I had secured a new hard drive.

Well, at this time I am working on the final edit of The Lost Forest and Charlotte still wants to do the Lovecraft story and she's now added The First Girl in the Moon to the to-do list.

Of course we do have a pretty cool looking design for the armature that is going to become the Elombah. With a little skin and a bit of money we might actually make the Last Voyage. The Lost Forest is a for sure to happen. Last Voyage is a maybe. But I'm serious looking at Girl in the Moon somewhere in the in between time. And all of these will end up being a part of the Johnny Jupiter story lines.

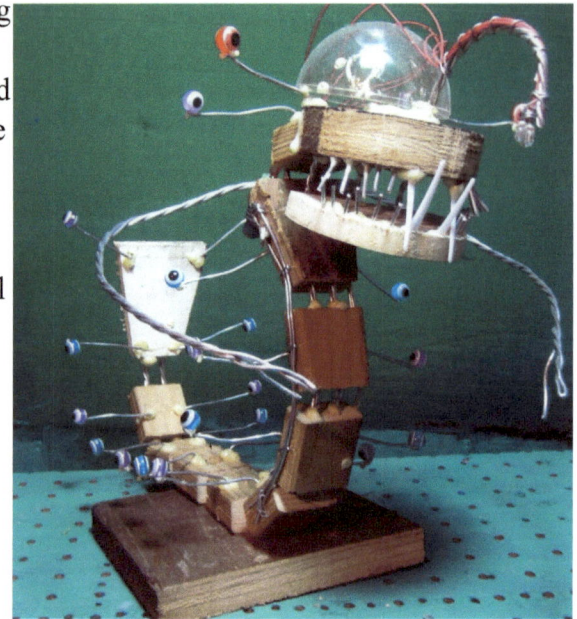

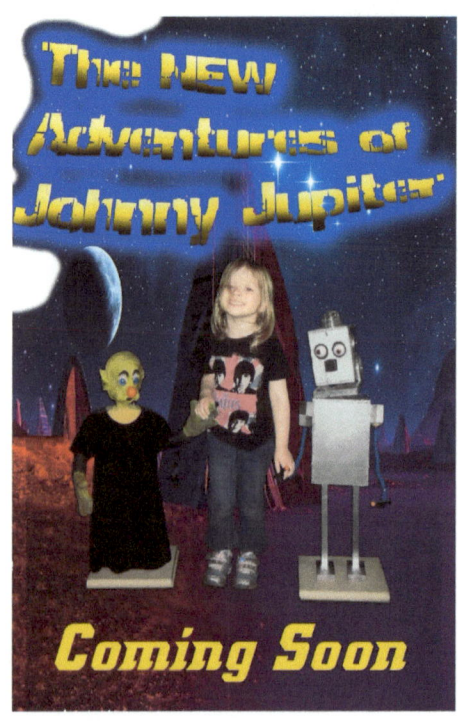

www.ingramcontent.com/pod-product-compliance
Lightning Source LLC
Chambersburg PA
CBHW051823210526
45473CB00005B/1714